KNOW YOUR RIGHTS DURING POLICE ENCOUNTERS

CARL DAVID CEDER, ESQ.

Speakeasy Publishing
73-03 Bell Blvd, #10
Oakland Gardens, NY 11364
www.speakeasypublishinginc.com

Ordering Information:

Quantity sales. Special discounts are available on quantity purchases by corporations, associations, and others. For details, contact the publisher at the address above.

Orders by U.S. trade bookstores and wholesalers. Please contact Speakeasy Publishing: Tel: (888) 991-2766 or visit www.speakeasypublishinginc.com.

Printed in the United States of America.

Published in 2023

ISBN: 978-1-951149-14-7

DEDICATION

This book is dedicated to the two most important men in my life: my father - Dennis Ceder - and my son, Benjamin Ceder. Without these two people, I don't know where I would be. My father was my hero and taught me how to work hard and be tenacious, but he also tempered it with being a consummate professional and a gentleman. My son is the reason I want to be the best person possible, both as a father and a lawyer. I strive to be a better attorney in many ways because I want him to be as proud of me as I was of my own father. I hope to never let him down. My beautiful son keeps me motivated and energized to try to set the best example for him to see how a man should be. I hope someday he will join me in the practice of law, as I believe there is no better job to have. My father taught me how to be a man that is honest and to always seek to do what is right. My dad passed away and, though he is gone, my son serves as a gentle reminder to always stay true to the beliefs he instilled in me. One of those beliefs is to be passionate about what you believe in. My father was a football coach and loved Vince Lombardi. I believe many of the examples he taught as a coach on the football field directly apply to being able to advocate as an effective trial attorney. This book is to the men in my life who make me strive every day to be the best version of myself that I can be.

"The difference between a successful person and others is not a lack of strength, not a lack of knowledge, but rather a lack of will."

—Vince Lombardi

DISCLAIMER

This publication is intended to be used for educational purposes only. No legal advice is being given, and no attorney-client relationship is intended to be created by reading this material. The author assumes no liability for any errors or omissions or for how this book or its contents are used or interpreted or for any consequences resulting directly or indirectly from the use of this book. For legal or any other advice, please consult an experienced attorney or the appropriate expert who is aware of the specific facts of your case and is knowledgeable of the law in your jurisdiction.

Ceder Law Firm
1611 K Avenue
Plano, Texas 75074
(469) 900 0000
www.CarlCederLaw.com
Carl@CederLaw.com

TESTIMONIALS

"Sandy and carl go above and beyond for their clients. I had a state jail felony for a wax pen, they were able to help me change my whole life around by getting me into the pretrial diversion program. I even had priors, which I personally feel like I would not have been able to be accepted into the program without their help! They have done so much for me to help me improve my life, I 100% recommend them to anyone in any kind of drug/alcohol charges! They have succeeded and helped me thrive in every single task or problem that has been thrown at me. Thank you so much, guys! I will refer to others, and will call again if I am ever in any trouble!"

—Anonymous

****

"When I first got into this situation, I was beyond scared. I had my son on the way of taking care of my girlfriend who was on bed rest. I met with Carl Ceder and he was upfront with the situation I was in. It was serious. This lawyer protected me to the fullest and got the best deal for me and it was even better than the outcome I was predicting. You can trust Carl Ceder and his paralegal Sandy. She is a very sweet lady who will walk you through everything while Carl focuses on the legal courtside. If your ever in need of a lawyer and don't know who to go with, choose this group they won't let you down!"

—Brent

****

"I was very pleased with the overall results with Carl. He walked me through the case with ease. He gave me worst-case scenarios but also showed me the light. Once my hearing was cleared he immediately initiated for me to be clear from my record. Thank you, Carl."

Amy

****

"I got a DWI in Collin county in December and called several lawyers. Sandy, Carl's paralegal, is so kind and informative and non-judgmental which helped throughout the stressful process. All I can say is do exactly what they say and you'll be just fine. Would definitely recommend them!"

—Anonymous

****

"I hired Carl Ceder to help my 13-year-old with a very serious issue. He represented my son better than I could have ever imagined. Our needs were put first, and I was treated as a friend rather than a number. My opinions were valued, and our doubts were always reassured. My nerves were calmed, and the process was always explained in detail. Carl fought hard for my son. He went above and beyond and did everything he could to ensure a great outcome. If I need an attorney in the future, he will be my first call. I couldn't have asked for a better attorney. Thank you, Carl!"

—Sandra

****

"Mr. Ceder was a very easy and direct attorney to have at my side for such a serious situation in my life. He was easy to contact and made his assistant Sandy just as easy to be able to get a hold of. He didn't try to extend the time it took to close my case out and have it dismissed. Mr. Ceder and his assistant did a great job of making sure I completed things that were necessary to have my case dismissed in a very timely manner and I am grateful for his professional courtesies and reminders. No beating around the bush here!! I am very satisfied!"

—Cynthia

****

TABLE OF CONTENTS

A Note From The Author

From the time I was a very young child, I wanted to be a criminal defense lawyer. A close family member got into some trouble and when I watched a lawyer handle the case, I made up my mind that I would one day grow up and make a living doing the same. I did not want to be just a lawyer; I wanted to practice criminal defense. I wanted to be someone who used my knowledge and skill to assist people during some of the most difficult times of their lives. I have never wavered from this intention to fight for the rights of others.

While many other criminal lawyers get their start working for the District Attorney's office to get trial experience, I'm proud of the fact that I have never worked to put someone in jail. Despite receiving opportunities to work as an ADA right out of law school, I have only represented individuals in court – never the state. That's because this isn't just a job for me – I am truly passionate about my calling.

I can state without reservation that my focus has always been on trying my best to achieve results in the courtroom solely for individuals and people. I truly believe from the bottom of my heart that the best legal advocate in court to defend a person accused of a crime is an attorney who has devoted their entire legal career to defending the rights of people, rather than someone who has spent any amount of time trying to work to put people in jail or prison.

As I said, practicing criminal law for me is my passion, and I feel that I truly can never learn enough about my craft. I am always trying to improve my knowledge, tweak something, and seek out answers to questions from others in the field who may be able to help increase my overall understanding of the law. To this end, I have kept a very precise notebook of copies of literally every successful result I have ever obtained throughout my legal career - including judgments of acquittals, dismissals, grand jury "no bills" of indictments, and more.

I feel, in many ways, that the practice of criminal law is my calling and not just my job, and I feel fortunate to be able to do this for a living. I am firmly committed to always trying to improve, to get better, and to assist in any way possible to elevate the perception of the criminal bar. With my practice, I have tried continuously to do my absolute best to effectively give the best legal advice possible to those I represent. I can honestly state I have done all within my power to constantly hone my skills to be as effective as possible as a trial advocate for those I represent in court.

About The Author

Carl David Ceder is a Texas trial attorney who has dedicated his practice to criminal defense. He has been licensed since 2008, has devoted his entire legal practice to defending the citizens accused, and is passionate about being their legal advocate in court. Quite literally since first obtaining his license to practice law, Carl immediately began the practice of criminal defense, with a particular emphasis on charges of DWI. He is very proud to say that he has never worked in any capacity to put people in jail and has only worked to defend and protect the rights of individuals in Texas.

Carl has extensive trial experience and has represented individual clients in a wide variety of legal matters in both state and federal court. From the very beginning of his practice, Carl decided DWI Defense would be his focal point and established a firm commitment to remaining on the cutting edge of the constantly shifting landscape of DWI laws.

The main focus of his practice is on DWI and other intoxication-related offense cases in Texas, especially in the regions in North Texas including Dallas County, Collin County, Denton County, Tarrant County, and Rockwall County. As a result of his determined desire to win, he has accumulated an extremely successful track record of results, with outcomes ranging from acquittals, dismissals, and reductions from the original offense to lesser offenses.

Carl David Ceder is Board Certified in Criminal Law by the Texas Board of Legal Specialization. Overall, less than one percent of all Texas lawyers are board certified in criminal law and very few have obtained this distinction without ever having worked as a prosecutor.

What's more, Carl has earned the American Chemical Society-Chemistry and the Law (ACS-CHAL) "Forensic-Lawyer" Scientist Designation. This designation is sponsored by ACS-CHAL and is approved for lawyers through Axion Analytical Labs in Chicago, IL. The ACS-CHAL Forensic Lawyer-Scientist Designation is awarded to lawyers who have met the rigorous criteria and have demonstrated their knowledge of forensic science. This designation is the highest form of scientific recognition available to lawyers. As a Forensic Lawyer-Scientist, Attorney Carl David Ceder can better understand and properly evaluate chemical and forensic evidence, especially as it pertains to blood alcohol concentration (BAC) test results in DWI cases, and also the effects that alcohol and other substances have on the human body.

In the courtroom, Carl has conducted a wide variety of criminal jury trials, at both the misdemeanor and felony levels, working hard to achieve a very high rate of success. Carl prides himself on being an aggressive trial attorney when the situation dictates, with over 50 felony and misdemeanor jury trials handled throughout his legal career. He has conducted criminal jury trials, as lead counsel, in 11 different counties in the State of Texas, and is always ready and willing to pick a jury on a moment's notice. Carl is proud of his track record of success with obtaining favorable results following jury trials and has obtained acquittals ("Not Guilty" verdicts) in numerous counties, including those counties which are commonly known to be the most notoriously "toughest on crime" in Texas.

Carl has devoted countless hours of training on subjects pertaining to various certifications and coursework specifically related to DWI, including with the National Highway Traffic Safety Administration (NHTSA) Standardized Field Sobriety Testing. He has obtained a certificate of completion for the NHTSA/International Association of Chiefs of Police (IACP) Standardized Field Sobriety Testing Instructor Course. He even frequently presents training to other attorneys for specific DWI trial methods and techniques.

On three separate occasions, Carl has completed and been awarded certificates of completion for the

NHTSA/International Association of Chiefs of Police (IACP) Standardized Field Sobriety Testing Practitioner Course (with two additional practitioner update courses beyond the original certificate of completion). He also obtained a certificate of completion for the NHTSA/International Association of Chiefs of Police (IACP) Advanced Drug Recognition Expert (DRE) course, qualified through the "ARIDE" Program (Advanced Roadside Impaired Driving Enforcement).

Carl also has obtained advanced training with a certificate of completion for the course, "Horizontal Gaze Nystagmus (HGN): Vision Science Perspectives", which is based on how to conduct the "HGN" Standardized Field Sobriety Test properly. He also obtained Breath Test Operator Certification by completing the "Breath Alcohol Technician Course" of the Intoxilyzer 5000EN, according to the United States Department of Transportation Code Federal Regulations 49 Part 40. Carl also has completed advanced coursework in the Intoxilyzer 9000, which is now the main evidential breath testing device used in Texas.

Attorney Carl David Ceder has been recognized by the Texas Criminal Defense Lawyers

Association (TCDLA) with the distinguished "DWI Trial Lawyer" Award, which recognizes those who exhibit a high standard to the practice of DWI Defense and who exhibit a strong devotion to developing the skill while showing an exceptionally standard of legal excellence.

Carl has been recognized every year from 2014 to 2020 as a Texas Rising Star Attorney in the field of "Criminal Defense" by the Texas Monthly Magazine. This achievement is only awarded to 2.5% of all attorneys and is a distinction only bestowed to those who undergo a rigorous peer selection process. Carl has been invited for inclusion each consecutive year from 2014-2020 for membership in the prestigious "The National Trial Lawyers' Top 100." Carl has also been included each consecutive year from 2014-2020 by the same organization as a member of the exclusive "The National Trial Lawyers' Top 40 Under 40" list. Selection into "The National Trial Lawyers' Top 100" and "Top 40" is an honor given to only a select group of lawyers for their superior skills and qualifications in their respective fields of law. Both are invitation-only organizations composed of the premier trial lawyers from each state who meet very stringent qualifications, and for attorneys who exemplify qualifications, trial results, and leadership as young lawyers.

What's more, Carl has been selected, in each consecutive year from 2014-2019 as a member of "The Nation's Top One Percent" by the National Association of Distinguished Counsel ("NADC"). The "NADC" is an organization dedicated to promoting the highest standards of legal excellence, with a mission to objectively recognize attorneys who elevate the standards of the Bar and provide a benchmark for other lawyers to emulate. Carl has also been awarded the "10 Best Client Satisfaction" award from the American Institute of Criminal Law Attorneys (AIOCLA) in 2014, 2015, 2016, 2017, 2018, 2019, and 2020. The AIOCLA recognizes the "10 Best" Attorneys for the State of Texas and is an impartial third-party Attorney rating service recognizing the excellence of fellow practitioners in the field of their chosen area of practicing law.

Carl is an active member of the Texas Criminal Defense Lawyers Association (TCDLA), the Dallas Criminal Defense Lawyers Association (DCDLA), the Collin County Bar Association, the Collin County Criminal Defense Lawyers Association (3CDLA), the Plano Bar Association, the National College of DUI Defense (NCDD), and is a "Founding Member" of the Driving Under The Influence Lawyers Association (DUIDLA). Carl is also admitted to practice in the United States Federal Courts of the Eastern, Western, and Northern Districts of Texas.

Carl received his Juris Doctorate Degree from the University of Houston Law Center in December of 2007, graduating in just under 27 months. He sat for, and successfully passed the Texas Bar examination earlier than most of his classmates and was admitted to the State Bar of Texas on May 2nd, 2008. Carl obtained a Bachelor of Business Administration in Finance in less than three years with a dual minor in Accounting and Management from the Red McCombs School of Business at the University of Texas at Austin.

Carl is a fifth-generation Texan and is proud to live in the state where he was born and raised. Carl graduated salutatorian (2nd out of 436 students) from Austin Lanier High School, and perhaps his proudest accomplishment is starting both ways on his varsity football team, including playing on the 1998 26-4A district champion Lanier Vikings. Carl is also the proud son of a former Austin area Texas High School Football Coach. He believes that many of the same fundamentals that lead to success on the football field (discipline, work ethic, and preparation) also apply to winning in the courtroom.

CHAPTER 1

AN INTRODUCTION TO LAW ENFORCEMENT ENCOUNTERS

The following pages are entirely meant to help inform the ordinary citizen who isn't familiar with their legal rights. Too many people are taken advantage of by various law enforcement officials because they either did not know their rights or were too afraid to exercise them.

In my line of work, I often tell people that honesty is rarely the best policy. The truth is, advising individuals on matters related to criminal defense is one of the few exceptions where this rationale is a good policy to follow. One must know their legal rights before one can properly exercise them.

The truth is, if the police make a mistake during the encounter, they will still go home to their families. Even though law enforcement officials are a necessity in society, they can equally make your life difficult and act with great authority under their police powers. Most are not engaged in the profession to "search and protect" to help out the community like Andy Griffith did as the Sheriff of Mayberry. Quite the opposite, they are not your friend but your opponent.

In this respect, police officers can and often are dangerous adversaries who know how to get what they want: arrests with as much evidence as possible to make them look good later in court. It is not the job of a police officer to educate or inform a person of what their rights are and how best to approach the rules of the system. So, in most scenarios, the police very much take advantage of the ignorance of the average citizen and their overall success in doing their job is ultimately measured by this major difference.

As a criminal defense attorney, I can personally attest to this fact. Most people get the education written here only AFTER a law enforcement encounter and with their first-hand experience quite literally in the criminal justice system. I believe that one shouldn't have to literally go to jail to get experience and understanding of how our laws work and how the police go about making arrests. It is wise to learn and understand the rules the police play with and, hopefully, you will never have to use this information.

The best part is that the process for achieving this is not complicated in the least. The most difficult hurdle to overcome is YOU!

Many people have an ingrained sense of cooperation, especially with the police. Many people also have an overwhelming urge to try to prove their innocence or talk their way out of an arrest or a situation. However, if you don't give them evidence and ammunition to work with, they cannot and will not be able to use it against you. It cannot be understated enough to fight this instinct and urge because it is precisely the contrary of how you will possibly achieve the objective it is used for – to avoid being arrested.

Our system of justice only works when both citizens and law enforcement officials alike have a thorough and comprehensive understanding of the scope of police power and the rights bestowed upon the people of this country. Not having this understanding has created an imbalance of power among the police that can lead to being bullied, pressured, or abused. It can also create unnecessary violence, tension, and an overall distrust of the people who are supposed to act as our protectors.

Many confrontations are avoidable and arrests can frequently be prevented. However, this preventative measure has to be predicated on your knowledge of the law and sticking to a script. While this book does have a lot of information that may seem overwhelming at a glance, the basic outline of this script is actually not hard to understand or follow.

The information you are about to read will not only keep you safe but will ensure the officer's safety, as well. Reading this book may very likely result in you avoiding arrest by the police one day. If everyone followed my advice, I would have to practice another type of law. Even so, I firmly believe that there is no safeguard or valid reason why these constitutional rights should be a secret to any citizen of this country.

This book will give you the proper information and guidance to understand what your fundamental constitutional rights are during all law enforcement encounters, the reasoning behind why there is no shame in asserting them, and will help you safeguard the rights our founding fathers died to protect.

There is a reason that lady justice is blind, and it is because justice requires transparency to be fair and equal. My perspective is that there is no benefit to keeping your constitutional rights afforded to you a secret. These rights were founded and established over hundreds of years by people who fought, and sometimes died, for the freedom we enjoy in our country. It is an absolute disservice to our country if the criminal justice system operates through an incredible imbalance of power by the police over the rights of American citizens.

This disproportionate and unequal system cannot operate effectively when only law enforcement officials have a fundamental and comprehensive understanding of the breadth and extensive scope of powers held by the police. As we are seeing today in current events, such an imbalance of power creates a justice system that pervades exploitation, tension, distrust, violence, abuse, and pressure on society and the world we live in as Americans.

The playing field only evens out when both sides know how the rules work and are applied. If this happens, it will lead to more effective and less intrusive policing which, in turn, will lead to the conviction of people who are actually guilty rather than the victimization of the innocent.

Police officers are trained and routinely attempt to exploit and capitalize on the inability of the average person to know, understand, and have the capability to properly articulate their rights. Thus, there is a compelling need to have ample safeguards in place to protect from police misconduct that occurs every day all around our country.

Unfortunately, the safeguards which exist to protect your rights are moot if one does not know or is unable to see how readily apparent and available they are to freely use. Usually, people don't know until it is too late whether they have been treated unfairly and are forced to learn the hard way how their rights were violated or taken advantage of.

Each section of this book attempts to deal with a separate and distinct legal issue as it pertains to an encounter with law enforcement, some of which will overlap. While it contains information on many facets and circumstances for how a situation like this can result, the advice given, when taken in context, is relatively easy and simple to follow - even if one believes the laws in the United States to be complex and complicated to understand.

This book will deal with defining the different types of police encounters. It will include scenarios that exist that many never believe they would have found themselves in, what to do in these scenarios, and meanwhile address the copious amounts of misconceptions, myths, and mistakes that I have seen throughout my legal career.

This book and information are not meant to be a criticism of law enforcement. There will always be police officers who behave in a rogue fashion and abuse their position of authority and power, but we can make it so that it is increasingly difficult for them to lure unsuspecting and unwitting targets.

The goal should always be to avoid police officers. You need to be aware of dangers and possible situations where you may fall victim to a crime in the same way that you need to be cognizant and aware of your constitutional and legal surroundings.

This advice is intended for those who never thought about what to do during a police encounter. If utilized correctly, it is my hope that this book will either help the reader avoid an arrest or, at the very least, help the reader with their case at court should they ever find themselves there. Simply put, police officers have the knowledge, are well-trained, and are educated. The public has the right to be equally educated.

This book will also detail what all people in power, including and especially police officers, know about the Criminal Justice System and how the "game" is played. It is true that EVERYONE who has the privilege to know how the criminal justice system and police operate WOULD NEVER advise their loved ones (or themselves) to waive their right to remain silent in the face of a criminal investigation.

We routinely see people in power, including politicians, police officers, government officials, etc. plead the 5th Amendment. Most of these people are officials in power. Police officers who have made a career and a living out of talking innocent people into waiving their right to remain silent will not do the same when faced with questions. Why should the average, ordinary citizen waive their right to remain silent, then? The answer is simple. **DO AS POLICE OFFICERS DO!** When in trouble, do not consent, do not give statements, ask for your right to counsel, and refuse to give any admissions whatsoever. PERIOD.

"Nobody of sound mind can dispute that there is something fundamentally wrong, and intrinsically corrupt, about a legal system that encourages police officers and prosecutors to do everything in their power to persuade you and your children (no matter how young or old) to "do the right thing" and talk – when they tell their own children the exact opposite."

— James Duane,

You Have the Right to Remain Innocent

CHAPTER 2

THE DIFFERENT TYPES OF LAW ENFORCEMENT ENCOUNTERS

By understanding and adopting the approach set forth in this book, you will minimize your chances of avoiding an arrest and possibly having to deal with law enforcement situations altogether. This advice is not set forth with the idealistic and unrealistic notion of saving society as a whole; instead, it is intended to possibly save you if you ever find yourself standing in front of a police officer with a badge and gun proudly displayed and handcuffs ready to use at any given time.

This information is intended to assist and advise individuals on how to act, speak, and behave in order to either not get arrested at all or to aid in their chances of having a successful result later in court. I have seen too many people who have suffered the consequences of not having the knowledge of how to react when encountering the police, and only learn what to do later after I represent them against the criminal accusation in court.

I took an oath when I passed the Texas Bar examination and swore to uphold the Constitution. The oath before being officially licensed to practice law as an attorney includes the following language (this is not the entirety of what it mandates): "I, Carl David Ceder, do solemnly swear that I will support the Constitutions of the United States, and of this State..."

This is an oath I take very seriously and it is central to why I am passionate about trying to ensure that our Constitution and the rights it enumerates are accessible to everyone. It is my belief that neither the Constitution, the law, the cases we rely on, nor our criminal justice system should only be understood and recognized by just an elite, privileged few. Rather, it should be readily available and easily accessible for everyone to understand and appreciate.

So, when putting all of this in place, it's helpful to start with an overview of the basics. Part of understanding the basics is to understand the three main types of law enforcement encounters: 1) A Consensual Encounter; 2) A Detention; 3) An Arrest.

1. Consensual Encounters

The first way one may interact with the police would be something termed a consensual encounter. It is viewed as a voluntary encounter because, in theory, it is consensual in nature and can be ended at any time. Police officers are just as free to go up to someone in the general public and start talking to them. However, you are free to ignore that officer, just as you are free to ignore anyone who approaches you in a public place.

During a consensual encounter, an individual has the right to just simply walk away, to not identify themselves, and one can even directly tell a police officer that they do not want to speak to them. A consensual encounter does not require any level of proof, such as reasonable suspicion or probable cause.

A consensual encounter would include a situation where an individual is approached by a police officer who initiates conversation and does not outwardly involve any show of force or authority, such as direct police commands, any form of force, or lights and sirens. For a consensual encounter to take place, there does not need to be any evidence or suspicion of a crime that has been or will occur.

However, there is a fine line distinguishing when one can exercise their right to ignore a police officer and walk away, or if the encounter is indeed detention. Ultimately, the best way to determine if a police officer is conducting a consensual encounter (or instead is conducting an investigatory stop or detention) is whether a reasonable person would not feel free to leave.

Thus, if there is any ambiguity in this regard, one should simply ask the question, "Am I free to leave?" And, if so, go on their way. Often, however, many people feel as if they are forced to acquiesce and feel compelled to stay, especially if the police officer is asking the person questions in a forceful manner, or in situations where there may be several other officers surrounding the individual.

Again, simply put - when in doubt, simply ask the officer, "Am I free to leave?" The bottom line is this, even without suspicion of wrongdoing, a police officer has the ability and is free to approach an individual and try to strike up a conversation just like anyone else could. However, unless you are being detained, you are equally as free to walk away as you would be with any other person coming up to you on the street.

2. Detention (Or Terry Stop)

The difference between a consensual encounter and investigative detention is very important to be able to differentiate as an individual's rights drastically change in each scenario.

Detention is by far the most common way people encounter law enforcement and it usually occurs during routine traffic stops. When an individual is pulled over for a traffic violation, it is classified as detention. Alternatively, a consensual encounter can turn into detention, or an investigatory stop, if an officer shows authority in a manner that restrains the individual's freedom of movement such that a reasonable person would feel compelled to comply.

In a detention, the police only need to have reasonable suspicion to stop (or detain) an individual. "Reasonable suspicion" is defined as a legal threshold that is less than probable cause (which is needed to effectuate an arrest or the issuance of a warrant), but also must be based on something that is more than just a "suspicion" or a "hunch."

The United States Supreme Court has described reasonable suspicion as something more than simply an "inchoate and unparticularized suspicion or hunch" and must be based on "specific and articulable facts" to suspect a person has been, is, or is about to be engaged in criminal activity. (Terry v. Ohio, 1968). As such, reasonable suspicion means that there was objectively reasonable evidence or circumstances to suspect and believe that an individual was involved in, or was about to be involved in a crime.

In short - if you are detained, you are not free to leave. This timeframe can vary depending upon the state or jurisdiction and/or based on the circumstances, but the United States Supreme Court has held that 20 minutes or so is a reasonable timeframe for detaining someone. In other words, a police officer cannot prolong detention longer than necessary (around 20 minutes) to develop the requisite level of probable cause needed to make an arrest or to effectuate a search.

In detention, you have to comply with just two things. If you are on foot, you have to comply with giving your name to identify yourself. If you refuse or give a false name, you can be charged with failure to ID. If you're in your vehicle and you are pulled over, you should roll down your window just enough and give your ID, your registration, and your insurance card.

3. Arrest

Detention can become an arrest if certain factors come into play. To arrest an individual, law enforcement officers need to have probable cause. "Probable cause" means that there is sufficient evidence to believe a person committed or is in the process of committing a crime. However, there can be a distinction between when someone actually knows they are being arrested, or if they possibly are being held as a "custodial arrest."

A "custodial" arrest would be a situation most typically thought of when people think about being arrested by the police. The term "custodial" refers to the suspect being in custody. This situation would be where a person is placed in handcuffs, detained, and taken to jail. (Though, it's important to note, you won't necessarily be put in handcuffs.) Usually, a custodial arrest means in some form or fashion, a law enforcement official has deprived an individual of their freedom of action in some significant way. However, a person could be under "custodial" arrest given certain factors which may exist, but that they are not aware of.

Legally speaking, an arrest actually occurs if a person is being questioned by a police officer and feels that they are not free to leave. If you are not free to leave, either because you've been given the verbal direction that you are not free to do so or because it is clear based on the situation, then it is an arrest even if you technically haven't been booked or read your Miranda rights.

What's more, an arrest can occur without an individual technically being arrested. Texas has somewhat of a higher standard for what actually constitutes an arrest than some other states. Texas law states that when an arrest occurs, some freedom of movement has to occur. Even if you're not under arrest, sometimes in a DWI stop, police will get you out of the car and put you in handcuffs. If this occurs, then a legal arrest has occurred because there is a restriction on the freedom of movement. It is no longer detention. There is a significant difference between arrest and detention. If a proper custodial arrest has occurred and an individual has not been properly read their Miranda rights, anything said subsequent to the arrest and before the Miranda rights are read would not be admissible later at trial.

CHAPTER 3

COMMON POLICE ENCOUNTERS

There are three main ways that individuals usually encounter police:

- **On Foot**

  Usually, this type of encounter occurs on the street.

- **In Their Vehicle**

This is the most common way for the average citizen to encounter an officer. This type accounts for approximately 52% of encounters with the police.

- **Inside the home**

Whether inside your own home or another place of residence, this is the third most common type of police encounter.

Below, you can find an overview of these three main encounters and your rights in each…

1. POLICE ENCOUNTERS ON FOOT

An officer is as free as any other citizen to conduct a "consensual encounter" and approach a person on the street to engage in a conversation. However, if one feels this is the case, they would be free to ignore any questions posed to them by the police officer. However, if a police officer has the requisite level of reasonable suspicion that one may have been involved in a crime, they can initiate lawful detention to investigate further. Though, of course, this reasonable suspicion has to be based on more than a mere hunch.

If a police officer initiates a detention on foot, they are legally permitted to conduct what is commonly referred to as a “Terry” frisk. A "Terry" frisk is a general pat-down of a person for the safety of the officer to ensure that the person does not have any weapons that could pose a danger. This is only justified as a protective search for weapons.

If this search is conducted - DO NOT RESIST. However, clearly communicate verbally that YOU DO NOT CONSENT TO ANY SEARCH OF YOUR PERSON OR PROPERTY. If the police officer goes beyond what is proper and reaches into a pocket, for example, and pulls out a piece of paper, it would likely be deemed an illegal search because this would be outside the permissible scope of the "Terry" pat-down.

Additionally, if a police officer conducts an arrest or places you in handcuffs, do not resist, argue, or attempt to run away to avoid the encounter. If the police officer asks a question, the only answer a person legally has to give is their legal name. If they persist further with questions, but they have not communicated that one is under arrest, the person should ask if they are free to leave. If the police officer says yes - then simply leave and walk away.

If the officer states that you are NOT free to leave – one should then ask if they are under arrest. If the police officer answers no, they are not under arrest – then the person should communicate back that they do not want to answer any questions, and inquire as to the reason for the detention. If they are unclear about whether it is a "consensual encounter" or a "detention", one should simply ask what the nature of the encounter is.

If it is a "consensual encounter", a person is well within their rights to walk away and cease any further interaction. If the police officer indicates it is detention based on reasonable suspicion, request permission to leave once the reason for the detention is completed. If it is communicated that you are under arrest, immediately invoke your right to remain silent and request to have an attorney present. Be absolutely clear that you refuse to answer any questions until you are afforded your right to legal counsel.

<u>SUMMARY: IF YOU ARE STOPPED ON THE STREET</u>

- **Stay calm, remain polite, and try to be as cool and collected as possible throughout the encounter.**
- **Do not attempt to run, evade, or otherwise try to elude the encounter if it is clear a law enforcement officer is attempting to initiate lawful detention.**
- **Do not try to run away if you are approached on the street.**

If you are unclear as to whether it is a consensual encounter or investigative detention, just ask.

- **Make no attempts to resist, obstruct the investigation, or argue about the details of the incident during the encounter.**

Trust me - it is a fruitless endeavor to try to do so even if you are indeed innocent of whatever they may try to charge or cite you with and even if you believe they are clearly violating your rights. You can deal with this later - trying to sort all this out during the encounter is a terrible idea.

- **Always keep your hands where the police can visibly see them.**

Always avoid putting your hands in your pockets. A police officer's initial reaction to a person reaching into their pocket or waistband is always to believe it is to reach for a weapon.

- **If you are not under arrest and the encounter is taking longer than you think is necessary, ask if you are free to leave.**

If they indicate that you are, simply and in a calm and silent fashion just walk away. If they convey you are under arrest, you have the legal right to inquire for what reason and under what authority. However, even if you disagree with their answer to this, remain compliant and docile. Comply with whatever request or demand they give you.

- **You have the right to remain silent, and once you clearly and verbally invoke this right, all questions should cease.**

On a similar token, you cannot be punished for refusing to answer questions when exercising your right to remain silent.

- **In most states, you must comply with at least giving your actual legal name to a police officer when they request it.**

There is no reason to try to avoid this or fight this battle. Simply identify yourself properly if asked.

- **ALWAYS AVOID GIVING VOLUNTARY CONSENT.**

You have the right to NOT consent to ALL search requests, whether it be on your person (your clothing), your belongings, or anywhere and anything else you may have control over.

- **A police officer is legally allowed to conduct a Terry "pat down" or "frisk" of your clothing if they suspect you may be carrying a weapon.**

If this is done, it is imperative that you DO NOT try to physically resist. However, you also can try to make sure they do not exceed the scope of this basic pat-down of your outer clothing.

You also should remember if they try to search any further, you have the absolute right to refuse consent for anything or anywhere else. If you do consent, it negates the necessity of them having the requirement of procuring a search warrant. NEVER CONSENT TO ADDITIONAL SEARCHES.

2. POLICE ENCOUNTERS IN YOUR VEHICLE

By far, the most common way people encounter the police is during routine traffic stops. Unfortunately, most people do not know their rights even when dealing with the police during these encounters, which results in many making mistakes during the encounter that could have otherwise been avoided.

A routine traffic stop is classified as a "detention" rather than a “consensual encounter”, thus one is not free to avoid having to interact with the police to avoid this encounter. It is imperative that an individual always comply. During a traffic stop, the only information a person has to give is their legal name, which can be done simply by just giving them a driver’s license, along with their proof of insurance and registration.

The police can initiate a traffic stop for any number of reasons. An individual should pull over immediately and safely to the side of the road, preferably into a private parking lot. After pulling over, turn your car off, take your keys out of the ignition, place them on the dashboard, and then wait for them to approach.

Make sure there is nothing in “plain-view” that can be seen anywhere in the vehicle that could be construed as contraband or illegal. If they do see something of this nature, it would give automatic probable cause to search the vehicle. It is a good idea to have the driver's license, proof of insurance, and registration ready when they approach the vehicle, and simply give these documents by rolling down the window enough so you can make sure they can properly take possession of them. After this, one should then simply place their hands on the steering wheel and say nothing else whatsoever.

If asked why you were pulled over, DO NOT GUESS. Often, if they do not already possess the requisite reasonable suspicion to conduct the traffic stop at this point, whatever guess you may state may possibly provide an additional reason to justify the detention. One is only required to give the identifying information listed above, such as the full legal name and required documents indicating your legal ability to operate a motor vehicle.

If the police officer requests that a person step from your vehicle, always comply with this request. However, remember to exercise your rights, including saying as little as possible to avoid making any incriminating statements. Do not consent to any search of your vehicle, your person, or anything else - even if you feel you have nothing to hide. There are no repercussions for you in refusing to consent to a search of your vehicle.

If they have probable cause to search, do not resist or argue when the search is being conducted. Let your attorney contest the legality of the search in court. If you feel you are being investigated for a charge of DWI (usually, an indicator is if you are asked how much alcohol have you consumed), politely refuse to answer any questions, refuse to perform any roadside field sobriety tests, and also refuse to give consent for any chemical specimen to be obtained (whether the request is either breath or blood).

Individuals who are most likely to be subject to an arrest during a traffic violation stop are those who are suspected of having some kind of contraband in the car. They usually stop people for any myriad of ticky-tack things that may or may not constitute a legal traffic violation. They are hoping to be able to do more than just write a ticket. They are more often than not hoping the routine traffic stop turns into something more exciting for them, such as an arrest and an outright confrontation.

Police officers score little points by simply writing a traffic citation, but they know these encounters are the best ways to make big arrests. The reason is simple: most crimes involve the use of a car. Those vehicles may contain drugs, guns, money, stolen merchandise, or an individual driving while intoxicated or even with a warrant out for their arrest. While encounters on the street may result in a misdemeanor offense, traffic stops are often the beginning of felony arrests.

Police officers spend months and years in intensive training totally devoted to the following: how to find people they deem to be criminals to question, fight, arrest, possibly shoot, and ultimately obtain enough evidence to secure a conviction. Police officers do not get promoted or obtain a pay raise by helping communities and neighborhoods stay peaceful. To most police officers, concern for the safety and well-being of citizens is not their chief objective when making a traffic stop, but instead is a by-product usually achieved through years of training and experience on the street.

Police officers, especially those on patrol, spend countless hours studying the various ways to conduct a lawful traffic stop. Many of the traffic laws in any given state are incredibly petty. Some of them are completely gray areas, such as driving carelessly or weaving within a lane of traffic. Aggressive patrol officers study the entire traffic code with great intensity, not because they care about people driving more safely, but because it is the way to stop more cars, write more tickets, and increase municipal revenue. It allows them to perform more searches of vehicles and ultimately gives them the ability to make more arrests.

Generally, the police officer will ask you if there is anything illegal in your vehicle. If you admit that there is, you have given them probable cause to search your car. If you deny that there is contraband, they will ask to search your vehicle. If you should agree to give consent to a search, regardless of what is in your vehicle, because consent is the overarching factor that would make an otherwise illegally obtained piece of evidence admissible in court, you were literally availing yourself of your best possible defense.

However, there is absolutely no purpose to make their job easier for them, so make them do their job and try to obtain a valid search warrant that authorizes a search. If they do suspect something, they can get a search warrant. You don't need to make their job easier for them. You want to know your rights and do not want to consent to a search of your vehicle, even if you believe that nothing would ever be found that would be illegal in your car.

Countless people have been arrested and still believe that same rationale. At that point, ask if you are under arrest or if you are free to leave. If the officer says you are free to leave, then you should leave. If you are under arrest, you should invoke your right to an attorney and invoke your right to remain silent.

A quick note: *I want to make it absolutely clear that if a police officer observes ANY traffic violation when someone is driving a vehicle and they initiate a traffic stop (this can be in a marked or unmarked vehicle), a person ABSOLUTELY MUST STOP. Technically speaking, when an officer observes an infraction when someone is driving, it is a criminal offense (most likely a class C misdemeanor traffic violation).*

It is advisable to stop as soon as possible in order to not commit further observable traffic violations. Their initial reason for the traffic stop may have been unfounded or based on a mistake, so you don't want to give them any additional reasons for the stop.

Un-Arrestable Offenses In Texas

There are only two "un-arrestable" offenses in Texas:

1. A traffic violation for speeding
2. Allegedly having an open container

If either of these is the only criminal offense alleged to have occurred, an officer CAN NOT LEGALLY MAKE AN ARREST.

All other infractions, even for minor traffic violations - such as changing a lane without signaling, driving with a broken taillight, etc. – virtually anything in the transportation code is considered a criminal offense and any police officer has the power and authority to effectuate an arrest.

However, it should be noted this is usually done only when an officer believes they may find something else in the vehicle, they believe the person is engaged in more serious criminal activity, or for some other reason to legally have the authority to investigate further. Regardless, if an officer asks someone to step out of their vehicle, a person ABSOLUTELY MUST and SHOULD comply.

Being Polite & Courteous – Even With The Threat Of Drug Dogs

Always be polite and courteous, even if threatened by a police officer calling drug dogs. In any traffic stop scenario, it goes without saying and is obvious that throughout the encounter - and with any police encounter for that matter - a person must remain polite. If not, it may cause a person who may otherwise just be cited for a minor infraction, such as simply getting a speeding ticket, into being charged with something more serious.

If an officer does ask someone to get out of the vehicle, the rights of an individual are the same. A person has the right to refuse to answer any questions, other than providing their legal name (which can be done by showing proper identification, such as a valid driver's license).

However, regardless of the actual intention of the police officer, a traffic stop can only be conducted for as long as necessary for them to complete whatever the initial purpose of the stop. This is because it falls under the category of a "detention" and not an "arrest").

In other words, if the officer suspects that drugs may be in the vehicle, but the person does not give their consent despite repeated requests by the officer to try and coerce obtaining permission to search, they cannot prolong the detention in an attempt to gain probable cause to conduct an investigation further.

Sometimes when consent is not given to search an officer may threaten to call for drug dogs to conduct a sniff of the vehicle. If this occurs, one should still maintain and be resolute in refusing to allow a search. It is also possible that the officer may try to prolong the detention in order to keep questioning or pressuring the person until probable cause may eventually develop to justify a search or an arrest. This underscores the very reason why one should NEVER consent to anything, including and especially to a search of a person's vehicle.

Traffic Stops, Search Warrants, & Plain View

If you know you are going to be pulled over, try to make sure there is nothing in "plain view" that can be seen and possibly thought to be illegal contraband by the officer when he or she approaches. Why? Think about this: people consume illegal narcotics all the time in their homes on a routine basis, and police officers just pass by every day. The reason for this is simple – the police cannot see them.

Because police officers are unable to see and observe someone at a residence, it prevents them from being allowed to initiate an investigation to make an arrest. Police generally cannot search your residence without a search warrant. On TV and in the movies, they make it seem like all police officers need to do is make a phone call to obtain a search warrant. Nothing is further from the truth, especially for police officers working patrol making traffic stops. In reality, it is quite difficult and time-consuming and is never a simple task.

To obtain a valid search warrant, a police officer must write up the reasons for believing there is probable cause for a warrant to search, present it to their superiors, and ultimately to a Judge who then has to review it to determine if it is with merit. The process actually can be quite an aggravation for most patrol officers and can take up the majority of their day or night of their shift. As such, unless something is in plain view in your vehicle when pulled over, the odds are the police officer won't do what is necessary to obtain a valid and legal search warrant.

Many people have mistaken and exaggerated notions about their privacy rights, the need for police to always have to get a search warrant, and the precedent needed to acquire one. Even more people are under the mistaken belief that the police cannot search them on the street or in their car, period. However, the reality is not that complicated.

Simply put, if you are doing or if you have something in your possession and it's in plain view of the police officer, they can generally conduct a legal search without the need for a warrant. Meanwhile, if the same person is doing the same activity inside their home and they are not doing so in plain view, a warrant is required.

SUMMARY: IF YOU ARE STOPPED IN YOUR CAR

- **Stay calm, remain polite, and try to be as cool and collected as possible throughout the encounter.**
- **Do not attempt to evade or otherwise try to elude detention if it is clear a law enforcement officer is attempting to initiate lawful detention.**

- **If you know that a police officer is attempting to pull you over, stop your car in the very first available safe place as quickly as possible.**

Once you park, turn the ignition of your car off, get the required documents ready that you know will be asked, open the window only enough so you can make sure you give the police officer the documents, and then place your hands on the steering wheel.

- **Try to make sure you ensure there is nothing in "plain view" that can be seen and possibly thought to be illegal contraband by the officer when he or she approaches.**
- **Upon request, show the police officer your valid driver's license, registration, and proof of insurance.**

Have your driver's license, proof of insurance, and registration ready when they approach the vehicle, and simply give these documents by rolling down your window enough so you can make sure they can properly take possession of them. Then place your hands on the steering wheel and say nothing else whatsoever. If asked why you were pulled over, do not guess.

- **Always keep your hands where the police can clearly see them by placing them visibly on the dashboard inside your vehicle.**

Always avoid putting your hands in various places or moving them around (whether inside or outside of the vehicle), and also avoid putting your hands in your pockets, as the initial reaction of a police officer is always to believe it is to reach for a weapon.

- **If you are not under arrest and the encounter is taking longer than you think is necessary, ask if you are free to leave.**

If they indicate that you are free to leave, simply drive away in a calm and silent fashion. If they convey you are under arrest, you have the legal right to inquire for what reason and under what authority. However, even if you disagree with their answer to this, remain compliant and docile, and comply with whatever request or demand they give you.

- **If the police officer asks you to step out of the vehicle, comply with this request.**

However, remember to exercise your rights, including saying as little as possible to avoid making any incriminating statements.

- **If an officer asks to look inside or to search the inside of your vehicle, POLITELY REFUSE.**

However, if the police officer has reason to believe that your car contains evidence of a crime, it can be searched without your consent. If this occurs, even if you disagree with what is being done, do not resist or react combatively. If it is an unlawful search, let your attorney attack the legality of it later in court.

- **If you feel you are being investigated for a charge of DWI, your rights are the same.**

Usually, an indicator of this type of investigation is if you are asked how much you have had to drink. Politely refuse to answer any questions, refuse to perform any roadside field sobriety tests, and also refuse to give consent for any chemical specimen to be obtained (whether the request is breath or blood).

- **Drivers and all other occupants of the vehicle possess the same absolute right to remain silent.**

If you are a passenger in the vehicle, and you feel there may be something strange occurring with the encounter, you can ask permission from the police officer if you are free to leave. If the officer says yes, either sit silently away from where the incident is occurring or calmly leave without saying anything or making any movements that may seem suspicious. Even if the officer says no to your request, you still have the right to remain silent, and you should invoke it if questions are posed directly to you.

3. Police Encounters In A Residence

What do you do if police officers show up at your home or place of residence? Aside from a few limited exceptions, the police need a valid search warrant to enter your home without your consent. Many mistakes are made by individuals when police randomly appear at someone's doorstep. If this happens, it is VERY important to ascertain whether they have a search warrant or not.

Many people have questions and concerns about what to do when a police officer randomly shows up at someone's door. If the police arrive at a person's residence, there is a HUGE distinction between if they have a search warrant or not. If the police arrive at someone's place of residence, regardless of whether they have a warrant or not, they must announce who they are. If they have a search warrant, under the "knock and announce" rule, they must state their authority to search (before physically forcing their way into the home).

If the police knock on someone's door for whatever reason, outside of certain circumstances, an individual absolutely has the right to refuse entry. The most important thing to note is that in most cases, the police are legally allowed to come to an individual's residence (house or an apartment) and knock on the door.

Additionally, the U.S. Supreme Court has ruled that "whether the person who knocks on the door and requests the opportunity to speak is a police officer or a private citizen, the occupant regardless has no obligation to open the door or to speak." Thus, any individual in this situation is absolutely not required to answer the door or talk to the police even when they are knocking at your door if they are not in possession of a valid search warrant.

What's more, one should NEVER CONSENT, under any circumstance, to a search of their home or place of residence. The 4th Amendment to the U.S. Constitution states that "a person has the right to be secure in their persons, houses, papers, and effects, against unreasonable searches and seizures." This effectively means that unless a police officer has a valid search warrant, they generally cannot enter a person's home without consent. However, it is important to note that if someone opens the door and allows entry to the police, consent has been given, even if not verbally expressed.

The U.S. Supreme Court has ruled that a person's place of residence (home, apartment, etc.) is entitled to maximum search protection. As a result, even if officers have probable cause to believe something illegal is occurring inside the residence, the 4th Amendment of the U.S. Constitution still requires police to get a signed and valid search warrant from a judge to legally enter and search.

An individual has the right to be secure in their own home, and the police do not have the right to invade that privacy without a valid search warrant. If the police do not have a valid search warrant, a person does not have any obligation to even open the door. If the police are at an individual's door, they can do nothing more than any other regular citizen is justified in doing. In fact, just remaining inside your home is not an obstruction of justice – it is actually a constitutional right afforded to everyone.

In the event a person does want to speak with the police to find out why they are there, a person can step outside and close their door, or speak to them through the door without actually opening it. If you leave your door open, and the police see or hear something that may give them probable cause to investigate, they would then be legally entitled to enter the residence without a search warrant.

An individual can also legally request for the police to leave if they cannot produce and show a valid search warrant. In this instance, if you are outside speaking with them and they do not have a search warrant, you can go back inside and close the door behind you and cease all communication. Regardless, always remember to clearly and without equivocation tell them, "No, you cannot come in. I do not consent to a search, and I politely will not answer any questions, especially without my attorney present."

In this scenario, it is important to understand that absent a valid search warrant in possession of the police when they are at your front door, be VERY clear about communicating that *you do not consent to any search whatsoever and you will not give your permission for any entry onto your property.*

One could also simply inform officers (assuming they DO NOT have a valid search warrant) that consent will not be given, but if they leave a card at the door with their contact information, you will have an attorney contact them to inquire about the reason for their presence.

During this process, it should be noted that the police are trained to intimidate and pressure you into giving them what they are looking for, and actually, in most cases, it is an attempt to gain consent to enter the premises. Do not let any of their tactics intimidate or scare you into thinking they have more power than they actually do. Stand your ground. Protect your rights. Without a valid search warrant, without an exigent circumstance, and without your consent - they do not have any power to legally enter your place of residence.

3rd Party Consent At Your Residence

The laws and rules involving 3rd-party consent are very ambiguous and vague. Generally, the most relevant factor is who has the main key control over the thing or place that is to be searched. Anyone can consent to a search as long as the officers reasonably believe, in good faith, the third person has control over the thing or place that is to be searched.

As a result, if the police come to your door and you have a roommate, or someone else present who gives consent to a search of the premises, the police can then search the entire premises (even without a search warrant). It also should be noted that the police can ask your spouse, partner, roommate, guest, visitor, etc. for consent onto premises or access to items, (such as a computer), even if those items are not listed in a warrant.

Third-party consent is valid in many scenarios when the person has some type of authority over the premises, such as if another person has joint access or control over the place to be searched. However, if one realizes that consent has been given without their permission or perhaps arrives subsequently and in the middle of the search, they should immediately revoke the consent clearly and unequivocally.

"Knock And Announce Rule"

If the police arrive at a person's home or place of residence, especially if they do have a valid search warrant, they must "knock and announce" who they are, whereby they must state their authority to search (before basically physically forcing their way into the home). The "knock and announce" rule is a requirement mandating that police cannot just break down someone's door in order to execute a search warrant before knocking to see if they will be able to allow entry.

Under the "knock and announce" rule, police officers have to first knock on the door, announce the legal authority with which they intend to search the premises, and then wait a reasonable amount of time before they can then forcibly enter. Under this concept, at least in theory, even officers who have a warrant that justifies entering into a home or residence must first announce themselves and their purpose before intruding.

In the event that you determine the police at the door likely do have a valid search warrant, you should ask to examine its contents to see what it lists. The search warrant should list your home and address, the reason for the search, and in all other respects, conform to the legal standards of what it should contain. One should examine closely what the warrant does list to ensure that police officers do not exceed the scope of the search, possibly to other areas of the home not specifically listed.

If they do announce they have a search warrant, it is important to NOT impede their investigation, and to remain calm and polite, because it is possible that a person could be arrested and charged with obstruction of justice. If the police come to your house and ask you to speak to them, even with a search warrant, you are not required to talk with them. You do not have to interact with them, and in fact, a person has absolutely no legal obligation to do so.

CHAPTER 4

TEXAS SEARCHES WARRANTS

Police officers are required to give you a copy of the search warrant, and as such, you are legally permitted to inspect its contents. So, what exactly is in a search warrant?

It must specifically list the items to be searched or the things to be seized. Article 18.04 of the Texas Code of Criminal Procedure lists the required "CONTENTS OF WARRANT" - which should list a description of the reason and cause for the search.

A search warrant issued under Article 18.04 of the Texas Code of Criminal Procedure must contain the following:

- That it runs in the name of "The State of Texas";
- That it identifies, as near as may be, that which is to be seized and name or describe, as near as may be, the person, place, or thing to be searched;
- That it commands any peace officer of the proper county to search forthwith the person, place, or thing named; that it be dated and signed by the magistrate; and;
- That the magistrate's name appears in clearly legible handwriting or typewritten form with the magistrate's signature.

Generally speaking, if the police are at your door and they communicate that they have a search warrant for the premises, you may first ask them to slide it under the door or mail slot for inspection. However, please note this likely will not stop them from entering and conducting the search.

Additionally, it is important that you do not interfere with the police when they are executing the search warrant. Officers can seize any contraband or other evidence of a crime they find while executing a warrant if found in the proper execution of the search warrant, even if the object isn't mentioned within the contents of the warrant. Officers can also take reasonable steps to protect themselves during a search, such as telling the occupants of the place to be searched to remain in a certain area and even handcuffing them.

How To Spot A Valid Search Warrant

If you find the police knocking at their door demanding entry, you are perfectly within your rights to ask if they have a valid search warrant that is signed by a judge. Conducting a search in a reasonable manner generally includes showing the occupant of the home a copy of the warrant upon request.

Under Article 18.06(b) of the Texas Code of Criminal Procedure, a police officer when executing a search warrant "shall present a copy of the warrant to the owner of the place, if he is present. If the owner of the place is not present but a person who is present is in possession of the place, the officer shall present a copy of the warrant to the person." So, it is imperative to first ask if the police officers have a valid search warrant.

If they do – they have to physically present it to the owner (or if not present, to one who is in possession of the place). Article 18.06(a) of the Texas Code of Criminal Procedure dictates that a search warrant of a residence must be executed within a reasonable period of time, which is usually within around three days of its issuance.

What "Knock and Announce" Means For You

The "knock and announce" rule is a legal mechanism that mandates that police are not authorized to immediately force entry (by breaking down a door) into someone's place of residence when exercising a search warrant.

Under the "knock and announce" rule, police need to knock on the door first, properly announce their authority to search the premises, and then wait a reasonable period of time before they may enter. Only after announcing their authority to enter by identifying themselves as police officers to execute a search warrant, and if an individual then denies or fails to allow entry into the residence, the police can then forcibly come in.

Article 18.06(b) of the Texas Code of Criminal Procedure states that a police officer, when executing a search warrant, "shall present a copy of the warrant to the owner of the place, if he is present. If the owner of the place is not present, but a person who is present is in possession of the place, the officer shall present a copy of the warrant to the person." So, it is imperative to first ask if the police officers have a valid search warrant. If they do – they have to physically present it to the owner (or if not present, to one who is in possession of the place).

The Police Do Have A Valid Search Warrant – What Next?

You do not have to assist law enforcement when they are conducting their search. You do not have to answer questions while law enforcement is searching. Again, it is important to do your best to NOT do anything the police would construe as obstruction of justice or tampering with evidence (such as flushing items down the toilet, trying to damage things so they cannot be identified, etc.). This in all likelihood would result in additional criminal charges being filed.

It is also important to inspect the contents of the search warrant (as noted previously) because often police officers will try to search for things outside the scope of the warrant. They may only search for specific items listed and in places specifically listed in the search warrant itself. In other words, they cannot just openly explore and search the entire home, all rooms, closets, etc. if it is not within the scope of the warrant.

Before opening the door, in fact, it is advisable to close all doors and closets, turn off all electronic devices, and move anything you wish to keep private from plain sight. If after the execution of the search warrant is conducted and an item is seized, a police officer perhaps sees something suspicious in a room or a closet, this can broaden the scope of the search. The search warrant, in all likelihood, does not apply to the entire house. However, anything in plain sight may be seized that appears to be illegal or obvious evidence of a crime.

After the search warrant is executed, before the police officer takes property from the place, they are required to prepare a written inventory of the property to be taken, and also legibly endorse their name on the inventory and present a copy of it to the owner or another person in possession of the property. If neither the owner nor a person in possession of the property is present when the officer executes the warrant, the officer shall leave a copy of the warrant and the inventory at the place.

Exceptions To Search Warrant Requirement

If you do not offer consent for a police officer to enter your place of residence, the only other way they can come to enter without a search warrant is through one of the following **exigent circumstances:**

1. If the police have probable cause to believe a crime is being committed or that someone is injured and needs help.
2. If the police can articulate that emergency aid is needed or they believe that someone inside is in need of assistance.
3. If the police believe someone is in physical danger and in need of help.

   (A common example of this may occur in domestic violence cases wherein the police are responding to a 911 call of domestic violence and they need to enter the home to possibly prevent someone from being injured.)

4. When officers are in "hot pursuit" chasing a suspect who has fled the scene of a crime and

they have reason to believe that the suspect entered into a home to hide or avoid detection.

5. If they believe that entering the home would prevent the destruction of evidence during an investigation.

This is only valid if officers can reasonably show that waiting on a search warrant would be impracticable. In these cases, they must demonstrate that by the time the search warrant is created and signed by a magistrate, the evidence in question could very well be destroyed.

<u>It is important to note:</u> Any exigent circumstance must be based on specific, articulable facts before a police officer can justify the intrusion into a person's residence because a warrantless search is presumptively deemed to be unreasonable.

If There Is No Search Warrant

If the police knock on someone's door, an individual has the right to refuse entry. An important note here is that the police are legally allowed to come to an individual's residence and knock on the door, just as anyone else would be free to do.

The United States Supreme Court has mandated that in these circumstances, the police are in no way prohibited from doing so. However, the court has also dictated that when law enforcement officers knock on a door without a valid search warrant, they can do no more than any private citizen might do.

Additionally, the U.S. Supreme Court has ruled that "whether the person who knocks on the door and requests the opportunity to speak is a police officer or a private citizen, the occupant regardless has no obligation to open the door or to speak." Thus, any individual in this situation is absolutely not required to answer the door or talk to the police even when they are knocking at your door if they are not in possession of a valid search warrant.

One should NEVER CONSENT, under any circumstance, to a search of their home or place of residence. The United States Supreme Court has long held and ruled that a person's place of residence (home, apartment, etc.) is entitled to the absolute maximum search protection.

The 4th Amendment to the U.S. Constitution states that "a person has the right to be secure in their persons, houses, papers, and effects, against unreasonable searches and seizures." This effectively means that unless a police officer has a valid search warrant, they generally cannot enter a person's home without consent.

However, if someone opens the door and allows entry to the police, consent has been given even if not verbally expressed. One has the best protection inside their home against illegal and unreasonable police intrusions and has the absolute right to be secure in their own home, and the police do not have the right to invade that privacy without a valid search warrant.

In fact, if the police do not have a valid search warrant, a person does not have any obligation to even open the door and can stay inside. If the police are at an individual's door, they can do nothing more than any other regular citizen is justified in doing.

In fact, just remaining inside your home is not an obstruction of justice – it is actually a constitutional right afforded to everyone. In the event a person does want to speak with the police to find out why they are there, a person can step outside and close their door. If you leave your door open, and the police see or hear something that may give them probable cause to investigate, in which case, the police would then be legally entitled to enter the residence without a search warrant.

Alternatively, you can choose to speak to the police through the door without actually opening it. An individual can also then legally request for officers to leave if they cannot produce and show you for inspection a valid search warrant. In this instance, in fact, if you are outside speaking with them, you can go back inside and close the door behind you and cease all communication.

Regardless, always remember to clearly convey to the police officers at the door "No, you cannot come in. I do not consent to a search, and I politely will not answer any questions, especially without my attorney present."

You must be VERY clear about communicating that you do not consent to any search whatsoever and you will not give your permission for any entry onto your property.

If you have information about a crime that you would like to share with investigating officers, either speak to them through the closed door (not a window), or over the phone, speaker, or intercom. NEVER ALLOW POLICE OFFICERS WITHOUT A SEARCH WARRANT INSIDE. While they may be persistent, insist, or plead - do not budge on this. You have control over your domicile, not the police, so keep them outside.

One could also simply inform warrantless officers that consent for entry will not be given, but if they leave a card at the door with their contact information, you will have an attorney contact them to inquire as to the reason for their presence. If they communicate that it is sounding suspicious, you might choose to explain that you are cleaning the house for guests, or that other people inside are sick with the flu.

You must remember that during this process, often trained and experienced police officers will attempt to look for ways to intimidate and pressure a person to gain consent to enter the premises. Do not let any of their tactics intimidate or scare you into thinking they have more power than they actually do. Stand your ground and protect your rights. Without a valid search warrant, without an exigent circumstance, and without your consent - they do not have any power to legally enter your place of residence.

CHAPTER 5

UNDER ARREST

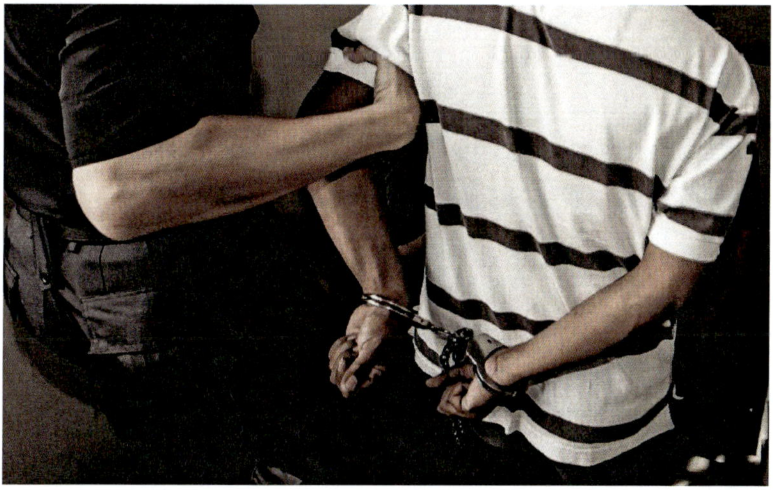

First things first: If you are being taken under arrest, make no attempts to resist the arrest, even if you believe the arrest is unlawful, not proper, or you feel it is unfair. Any issues surrounding the legality of the situation should be addressed by your lawyer later on - not by struggling against law enforcement in the moment.

Know Your Basic Rights

If you are arrested for any crime, it is imperative that you understand that you should always invoke your right to remain silent and request to speak to an attorney before even considering giving any answers to questions they may try to ask. Be clear and unequivocal with both requests, which should then terminate or cease any further questioning and interrogation. You then should directly ask why you are under arrest and try to say as little as possible while doing this. Hopefully, the police officer will talk and make a statement that could be used to your benefit later in court.

Being put under arrest is a very scary and confusing experience to go through. However, you must remember this *at all costs*: You must avoid being confrontational or rude, and you must avoid doing anything that could be remotely construed as physically resisting or being aggressive toward the officer. Any act of verbal or physical resistance or aggression could give the arresting officers grounds to charge you with the additional criminal offense of assault on a public servant and/or resisting arrest.

Of course, you have the right to inquire why the police officer is demanding you to go with them –

and if you are not under arrest, then you do not have to go with the police, nor should you. However, if you are placed under arrest, a police officer should tell you the reason why you were arrested. If you have been arrested and charged with a criminal charge, you do not have to answer police questions posed to you.

It's also helpful to know that an arresting officer usually will not inform you of your right to remain silent unless they have decided to charge you with a formal criminal offense. Some of the more shrewd police officers will occasionally even hold off on making an actual arrest (and therefore can wait to also give you the Miranda warnings) even though he or she already has the requisite level of probable cause to effectuate a proper and legal arrest.

In these situations, the officer will usually try to postpone making the full arrest in order to obtain more evidence from a talkative detainee - someone who usually doesn't realize that they have the right to not answer questions and the right to silence. The adage "loose lips sink ships" certainly applies here in a very significant way. Once the suspect is actually arrested and Mirandized, the officer knows the likelihood of being able to wheedle even small tidbits of information is usually not going to happen.

Finally, remember that a police officer is only allowed to use 'reasonable force' to carry out their job. All you have to do is stay as cool, calm, and collected as possible. Then, you can talk to a lawyer later about what you can do if you think the arrest was unfair or wrong or the police injured you.

General Rules When Being Placed Under Arrest

- **Be Polite.**

This is probably Rule #1 and perhaps the most important rule of thumb overall. Being rude, argumentative, or combative with the officer will get you absolutely nowhere. What's more, judges and Juries usually will hold this against an individual, and it could also lead to the officer getting peeved and charging you with additional offenses he might not have had you treated him or her with respect.

Always try your best to stay calm, polite, and courteous - even if the police officers are not treating you with the same respect. Being arrested is a nerve-racking experience, no doubt - but do your best to keep yourself in check and in control, both with what you verbally say and even with your body language.

Even when refusing, it is very wise to **always** be polite, often this in and of itself can prevent the situation from getting worse. I also believe it is perceived positively if you insert "please" and "thank you" when you communicate with them, even when conveying something like how you will not consent to a search, or when you exercise your right to remain silent or your right to an attorney.

- **Realize that you are likely being filmed and/or your audio is being recorded.**

The less you say, the better. Do not say anything that would possibly portray you in a negative light later to a jury or a judge in a hearing or a trial.

- **Do not argue, beg, physically resist, or verbally abuse the police officers.**

Regardless of how the police are treating you, make no attempts to resist the arrest – even if you believe the arrest is unlawful, not proper, or you feel it is unfair.

- **Make any necessary preparations for your family and for personal affairs if you believe an arrest is imminent.**

For this reason, it's important to try and commit to memory any relevant numbers of points of contact, most specifically, the phone number of your attorney.

If you have children with you, you can ask the police to call a family member or friend before they take you away.

If you take medication, try to make sure you have everything ready to document once at the jail: the proper medication, when it should be administered, etc.

- **Verbalize how you do not intend to physically resist the arrest but do state**

verbally and aloud your request to exercise your right to remain silent and make a request for legal counsel immediately.

Make no attempts to give explanations, excuses, or reasons for anything – especially anything related to the incident that is connected to the arrest. All attempts to talk your way out of this will fall on deaf ears, and it will no doubt be construed in some way by the arresting officers like you were trying to avoid the arrest because you knew you were guilty.

Don't play their game. You have the right to remain silent, use it. Let your attorney make whatever argument you have in court – where it would matter most. If necessary, verbally repeat "I DO NOT WISH TO SPEAK OR SAY ANYTHING UNTIL AN ATTORNEY IS PRESENT."

- **Never consent to any search. Period.**

Whether officers ask to search your home, your vehicle, your person, etc. – do not consent, even if you believe you have nothing to hide.

- **Even if you have not been read your Miranda rights, still invoke your right to remain silent and your right to have an attorney present.**

Do not say or talk to anyone else at the scene, in the squad car, or at the jail. Once at the jail and during the booking process, you are required to give basic information about yourself such as your name, your address, your date of birth, etc. However, beyond this basic information, always remember that you have the right to remain silent – so use it!

Say it out loud if you want to – this could be beneficial in that if others hear you express your intent to remain silent and to have your right to legal counsel, it cannot be misinterpreted later that you never made such a request.

- **Do not make any jail phone calls that can possibly be incriminating.**

If you call anyone, call someone to help assist with your jail release or call an attorney. Say as little as possible and discuss nothing even remotely related to the incident

Usually, you will be allowed to make at least one phone call, and sometimes, they allow arrested individuals to make several. BE CAREFUL. Always operate on the assumption that the police are listening or recording all of your conversations - because they usually do.

It is also advisable while in custody at the jail, only make a call to your attorney. The police cannot listen to or record any conversations that are shielded by the attorney-client privilege.

- **Wait to discuss or decide on anything related to your case until you have an attorney present.**

Do not discuss or talk to anyone about any details of your case, especially without the physical presence of your attorney. Do not make any admissions, statements, or answer any questions.

Do not make any decisions at all, even remotely related to your case, and do not even engage in casual conversation with anyone at the jail. If an individual or an entity persists in trying to make you do so, make it abundantly clear you will not do anything, AT ALL, without the direct advice and legal counsel from your attorney.

Again, never discuss **anything** even remotely related to your arrest or your case without your lawyer present. Do not talk to police officers, individuals from the district attorney's office, etc., even if they convey how they are trying to help you in some manner.

Always remember that anything you say can and, most likely, will be used against you later in court. Insist that this should only be done by and through your attorney, and specifically request that nothing of this nature be done without first speaking with your attorney.

- **Do not sign anything.**

Do not sign anything without a lawyer present who can review the contents of the document. You may be waiving some or all of your rights or you may be making an admission or confessing to a crime.

- **Ask for any strange or unusual conduct to be reported in the police log.**

You will be handcuffed, searched, photographed, and fingerprinted for most offenses. Once at the precinct, you should be searched by an officer of the same gender or of the gender you request. If this does not happen, ask the police to explain why in their police log.

And remember...

- Above all else, do not interfere, obstruct, or impede the job of whatever law enforcement official you encounter.
- Always give your correct legal name, and never give false documents to any law enforcement official.
- If you believe something was amiss or the behavior was inappropriate, try to remember the details of the encounter and make an official complaint if you feel that your rights were violated in any way whatsoever.

CHAPTER 6

COMMON MISTAKES MADE AFTER BEING ARRESTED

Without question, the most common mistake people make in encounters with law enforcement officials is talking too much. In the movie, The Judge, there is a scene where Robert Downey, Jr's character interrupts a confession that his father is voluntarily providing by saying a line that is one of my favorites: "Those who do not talk, WALK."

You have to remember, police officers are good at what they do and are very skilled at getting the information they are seeking from people (who usually are totally unsuspecting). Citizens often feel intimidated by the authority of police officers and law enforcement officials and usually end up saying WAY more than they should. Sometimes, people talk to police officers because they genuinely believe they will be able to explain what happened, effectively attempting to talk their way out of a situation of being arrested - **but nothing could be further from the truth**.

If the police are planning to arrest you, they're going to do so whether you give a statement to them or not. Many times, when people do give statements to the police, they feel like they can explain themselves, which will justify their actions, and the police officer after hearing whatever is said, will identify or agree with them and why something may have been done. Unfortunately, this rarely has the exact opposite effect and provides the exact evidence needed to convict you of the charge.

Also, many people simply do not know how the system works, so they feel that if they are cooperative and do everything the police are asking and requesting of them, all will be okay. Most people are very compliant because we are taught from a young age to respect police officers and people in positions of authority. As a result, if a person has never encountered the police, they will almost certainly say more than they should simply because they are trying to be cooperative and polite. This is why I have a passion for trying to appraise the otherwise unassuming public.

I've personally represented clients who have hired me for a criminal charge and I advise them on how to interact if they may find themselves in a position where they may be arrested again. More than on a few occasions previous clients of mine every now and then will sometimes find themselves in the position of having to deal with law enforcement again, but because of the knowledge and information I try to give to them when we first worked together on the previous case, usually, they are able to handle it in a better fashion, making it far less difficult to defend their case later in court.

CHAPTER 7

ALWAYS REMEMBER: NEVER CONSENT!

This is true regardless of the law enforcement encounter, whether it be on foot, in your car, at home, and whether it is a consensual encounter, an investigative detention, or an arrest. If you know and are sure you will be or are already placed under arrest, it is absolutely crucial to immediately exercise your right to remain silent and convey to the arresting officer how you would like to immediately invoke your right to have an attorney present with you.

Always be polite, calm, cool, and courteous when invoking both of these rights, but make it straightforward and absolutely clear.

In any police encounter, the main rules to follow, beyond all else, are the following:

1. Always be polite and courteous;
2. Do not make any admissions or give any statements;
3. NEVER GIVE YOUR CONSENT!

If asked for voluntary consent to search anything – your person, your vehicle, your residence – even if you fully believe you have nothing to hide, still clearly and directly state that you are not giving your consent.

In general, the more you talk, the higher the probability you may say something that could lead to further investigation. I have personally handled numerous criminal cases where people I have represented have, quite literally, talked their way into a conviction. This is especially true with cases where an individual is under investigation for a Driving While Intoxicated charge.

This remains true of people who give voluntary consent to search, believing they had nothing to hide, and also under the mistaken belief that if you cooperate with law enforcement, it will be in your overall best interest. I have seen countless individuals arrested and charged with a criminal offense by giving their consent when asked by a police officer, and had they not done so and politely declined consent, they likely would have been able to avoid being arrested and charged with a crime in the first place!

There is an old saying that comes to mind for me, *"Fish are caught only because they open their mouths."* Thus, always be polite - but keep your mouth closed, say as little as possible, and make it clear that at no point will you give your voluntary consent to search whatever place or thing is being asked of you.

If it is the case where the police officer believes they have probable cause to search, still make clear your position that you do not consent to the search, but keep in mind that if they proceed nonetheless, DO NOT interfere with them in the performance of their duties. If this occurs, record them with your phone if you can, or try to have a witness audibly hear you tell the officer how you are making it clear and know how you did not give your consent to search. The bottom line is there is no real advantage to consenting to any form of a search of a place or thing. However, there are a myriad of ways in which it could backfire, and lead to a possible arrest for a criminal offense. Therefore, ALWAYS, ALWAYS, ALWAYS REFUSE CONSENT if asked by any law enforcement official.

The reality is that when a police officer is investigating a scene or even during a routine traffic stop, law enforcement officials rely heavily on the public's overwhelming desire to have the confrontation end as quickly as possible. Most people will do whatever is necessary if it will lead to the police officer leaving them alone. While giving consent may lead to a shorter police interaction, you should never forfeit your rights, (and possibly your liberty and freedom), for the promise of expediency.

1. How Is Consent Usually Gained?

Officers are good at what they do. They usually will ask something like this: "You don't have anything illegal in here, do you?" If you say yes, it gives them probable cause to search. If you say no, the follow-up question will be something to the effect of: "Then you don't mind if we search your car, do you?" Most people try to be compliant with the police, and the natural response of a common person is to not be combative. Thus, most people respond back, "No officer, of course, I don't mind if you search my vehicle." This is very often true even when someone knows there is something illegal that will be found inside a vehicle.

Most people do not have the mindset to respond in the following manner: "No, officer – I do not have anything illegal in here, and I have nothing to hide. However, I absolutely do not give you my permission or consent to search either my person or my vehicle."

It is important to communicate this politely – but also to be firm and do not waver. If it is a traffic stop, the officer can only detain a person as long as necessary to effectuate whatever reason it is for why they pulled the person over in the first place. A prolonged detention results in the encounter being an arrest, and if this occurs, it likely will be deemed a prolonged detention later in court. This means that, if so, whatever incriminating evidence was obtained by the police officer will likely be ruled as inadmissible in court.

Often, people give their consent to search because they genuinely believe they have nothing to hide. However, often people are shocked to discover they can be arrested for things they did not have knowledge were illegal. For example, a mother who carpools her children and other neighborhood kids to school in the morning, may not have any knowledge if one of the kids happens to leave some of their prescription ADHD, anxiety, or antidepressant medication in her car. Kids often carry these to school and have a valid prescription, but they very easily could leave them behind inadvertently in a car when transported to school. If the mother consents to a search of the vehicle, and perhaps one of the children mistakenly drops some of the pills on the ground and cannot produce a valid prescription for the medication for herself, she very well could be arrested for possession of a controlled substance.

CHAPTER 8

THE "MAGIC WORDS"

To put yourself in the best possible position to properly counter all police and law enforcement tricks and tactics, one should **know** and **memorize** the "MAGIC WORDS" below. If you feel unsure of what you should do during any encounter with law enforcement or the police, simply just say the following. This concept applies regardless of the situation or scenario - whether if on the street, in your vehicle, after a traffic stop, at your home or place of residence, and even if you are at the police station after agreeing to give a statement about an alleged incident - politely and calmly recite the following "magic words" over and over again to the police officer conducting the investigation.

THE "MAGIC WORDS" APPLIED

1. "Officer, Am I Under Arrest?"

If the answer to this question is NO, then immediately proceed to #2 below.

However, if the officer answers in the affirmative and responds YES, then you are under arrest. Proceed to #3, #4, and #5. below.

At this point, you should then immediately respond back in a direct and clear fashion that you now wish to invoke your constitutional right to remain silent and do you want to answer any further questions without the advice of legal counsel, and then also promptly request your right to have a lawyer present. Say nothing else, at this point, beyond communicating to the officer your correct legal name and perhaps just minimal basic facts usually asked during the booking process.

2. "Am I Free To Leave, Officer?"

If the officer responds in the affirmative to the question – "Am I free to leave?" – and therefore, the answer is YES, you are free to leave, and so you should do just that - LEAVE!

If the officer responds to the question – "Am I free to leave?" – and the answer is NO, indicating that you are NOT free to leave, then politely inquire by asking, "Why exactly are you detaining me, Officer?" To be able to legally effectuate a detention, an officer must have reasonable suspicion of your involvement in some type of criminal offense, and it has to be based on more than a mere hunch or upon a vague suspicion.

Therefore, if the answer is NO, you are likely being detained, and thus, a "detention" likely has occurred – and the interaction is no longer a consensual encounter if it was one at some point previously. If the officer remarks that you are not free to leave, but yet, you are not under arrest - politely request the reason for the detention and ask permission to leave once he completes whatever purpose it was for which he initially initiated the investigative detention in the first place. If this is the situation, remain polite and calm, and simply wait for him to conduct the reason for the detention. Once this is complete - then LEAVE.

3. "I Do Not Consent To Any Searches."
4. I Invoke My Right To Remain Silent.
5. I Invoke My Right To Have Legal Counsel Present

Magic Words Summary:

1. "AM I FREE TO LEAVE?"
2. "AM I UNDER ARREST?"
3. "I DO NOT CONSENT TO ANY SEARCHES."
4. "I INVOKE MY RIGHT TO REMAIN SILENT."
5. "I INVOKE MY RIGHT TO HAVE LEGAL COUNSEL PRESENT."

General Thoughts On Law Enforcement Encounters

This content is entirely meant to help inform the ordinary citizen what their legal rights are who aren't familiar with the system. I have seen too many people taken advantage of by various law enforcement officials because they either did not know their rights or were too afraid to exercise them.

In my line of work, I often tell people I work with how honesty is almost never the best policy. Advising people on matters related to criminal defense is one of the few exceptions where this rationale is a good rule of thumb to follow.

For example, my father was the absolute most honest person I had ever known. When I was a young attorney, he was driving me one time when I was sick with the flu to Houston. A police officer stopped us for a reason that I cannot recall, but I can vividly remember what transpired next. Since I was sick with the flu, my seat was reclined back as we were driving on the highway, and because of this, I did not have my seatbelt on. Once we were pulled over, I immediately instructed my father to not say anything and to let me handle it and do all the talking – I knew my father was someone incapable of telling a lie.

The police officer came up to my passenger side window, I then rolled down the window, and before I could get a word out of my mouth, my father leaned over me and stuck his head out of the window, blurting out, "Did you pull us over because my son was not wearing a seatbelt?" I was astonished, and I looked at him in shock. I will also never forget the look on the police officer's face. He gave a half smile, probably surprised that someone would be so honest so fast, and he said, "Nooo... But, I suppose now I'll write a citation for the seatbelt violation as well."

My father was just so anxious and scared, it was his first reaction just to blurt out the last thing he really should have or was required to. This is a textbook example of a person trying to be honest, nice, and attempting to do the right thing – but it ended up causing additional trouble.

This story is a small microcosm of overall dealings with the police and law enforcement, but it does reinforce how in my line of work, the truth is simple: honesty is almost never the best policy. I don't think I can recall any scenario where a person has been better off attempting to cooperate as much as possible during an encounter with law enforcement and it has to be to their advantage.

Do As Police Officers Do!

One should do what police officers do when arrested for a crime. They impart the same information contained in this book to their children, loved ones, and friends. Not once have I ever met anyone in law enforcement or who has a parent or close friend who would do differently than what the essence of this book describes. Almost universally, it is known that if the child of a police officer is ever approached by a law enforcement official, they have been instructed previously to call someone else first (either the parent who works in law enforcement, an attorney, etc.), and all have been told regardless of the circumstances to never agree to voluntarily talk to the police.

They have also been instructed to never agree to a search, to never consent, and how to do a cursory function of properly exercising their rights. Everyone who is privileged enough to know the criminal justice system operates in the United States of America would never impart the advice to waive their right to remain silent if under investigation for anything related to a crime. We routinely see people who hold positions of power and authority, such as police officers, politicians, current or former prosecuting attorneys, and other government officials, exercise their constitutional rights, such as invoking their 5th Amendment right when refusing to answer questions. Many of these people have made a career out of doing just the opposite to people by convincing them to waive their right to remain silent to answer questions posed designed entirely to incriminate.

However, when the tables turn, and the questions are posed back at them, they will not reciprocate in kind and will do the exact opposite of what they have so many times talked people into doing. If you think about this, there is something inherently wrong and fundamentally corrupt about a system that allows police officers and prosecutors to do all within their power to persuade and convince someone to waive their right and talk to them, most of the time by employing very deceptive means when doing so. However, even though these same people countless times have argued with people to do the right thing and talk, or that it will be better for them to discuss with them when they tell their children (or would do so themselves) to do exactly the opposite of this when faced with a similar situation.

Our criminal justice system intrinsically has a double standard so grossly disproportionate where only those who are in the know stand to benefit on how to best protect and preserve their rights in a legal system that otherwise is predicated on taking advantage of the ignorance and good intentions of everyone else who, in contrast, are completely in the dark and blindly follow bad advice that is always entirely to their detriment. Anyone possibly can find themselves arrested or under criminal investigation and will be asked by someone in law enforcement to answer a few questions just to help clear things up. Unless prepared, this moment will come without warning to people or to someone they love, like their children. This usually is a turning point in the life of a person, and what is said and what occurs can seriously alter their future and life forever.

When this happens, unless one knows how to counter the position they are in with knowledge to combat strategy designed to extricate information to convict of a crime, the only advice a person usually obtains comes from a police officer who has the opposite of their best interest in mind, but nonetheless will convincingly lie to their face without any hesitation or pause, claiming they are looking out for them and falsely represent they have good intentions to help. The police who employ such methods have had extensive training in doing so and have been practicing and perfecting the same lie for years in order to be the most deceptive to achieve their objective.

I once heard a former police officer speak, who is retired and now works as a criminal investigator for criminal defense attorneys. He said he used to laugh with his police friends at how utterly stupid most of the people he arrested were, and likewise how utterly quick and easy it was for him to get them to waive their afforded constitutional rights. He mentioned how if everyone he investigated did exactly what almost every law enforcement official would do if placed in the same situation, his job would have been incredibly difficult and close to impossible. When he pulled someone over, he rarely, if ever, cared about the actual traffic infraction itself, but instead always hoped it would escalate into another, more serious crime, such as a DWI or a felony drug arrest. He was taught at the academy when he first started in his career to ask questions to prolong the stop with the hope it would turn into some type of admission to probe further.

In fact, he had a routine – that worked almost every time – to question the person about unrelated things, most of the time at least with the goal of obtaining consent, or establishing probable cause, to conduct a search of the vehicle. He listed an example of using a question to justify a DWI investigation by asking if the person had been drinking, or if they had been at a party or a bar. Almost without fail the person would answer to the effect of explaining how they had been drinking, where they came from, or other details that seemed totally benign in nature to the individual pulled over.

He employed this tactic to prolong the length and duration of the stop beyond what is legal for a traffic stop, and said the reasoning for why one should always refuse to answer any questions is entirely based on how usually the response given to the question asked is just what he had hoped to get. The answer given is always considered an admission of guilt in some form or fashion, and just gives them further reason to further justify the encounter. He said in all of his years as a police officer he could not recall a single instance, not even once, where it served to help the individual by engaging in the conversation – because his mind was made up with what he was going to do regardless of the answer.

Every year, throughout the country and in every major city in America, law enforcement officials get arrested for a myriad of different crimes, most commonly for charges of DWI (or "DUI"), assault, domestic violence, sex crimes, accepting bribes, drug charges, and also for stealing money or drugs from suspects. Even more who are not arrested are subject to very tough internal affairs investigations by their own respective department.

But if a police officer in any of these situations is interrogated or arrested, do you think they try to talk their way out of it? Therefore, perhaps the wisest advice I can give to anyone is to **do what police officers do**, which is almost always to **shut their mouths** as tight as possible and **lawyer up immediately**.

If it's an internal investigation into something they did while on the job, they not only hire an experienced criminal defense attorney to represent them in any proceedings, but also to show up for anything where they are required to be present with a union representative. Simply put, police officers are extremely savvy and are intimately familiar with the criminal justice system and how it works. They never would appear for any form of questioning without an attorney to protect them, as they know that any statement they make can be used against them, regardless of how benign it may seem, and will not give information for free without something contemplated in exchange.

When it comes to simply contemplating what to do in any law enforcement encounter, it is smart to look at news around the world and see how those who work in law enforcement conduct handling the situation. You never read about a police officer who gets arrested or is subject to a professional inquiry about their job as a police officer without an attorney present and by their side. It is why, in large part, almost all those in law enforcement usually do not have charges brought against them, and when they do, they have an overwhelming rate of either getting the charge dismissed, reduced, or found "Not Guilty" at a trial.

Main Points To Consider – Summary Of Your Rights

- You have the right to remain silent. If you want to properly invoke this right, you must properly exercise it by verbally expressing it out loud.
- You have the right to refuse to give any and all voluntary consent of your person, your vehicle, and inside your home or place of residence.
- Memorize the "Magic Words": If you are not under arrest, **ask the police officer if you are free to leave.** If you may leave, then do so calmly and quietly. If they respond that you are not free to leave, **ask if you are under arrest.** If they say you are, then **invoke your right to remain silent** and **your right to have an attorney present.** If they say you are not under arrest, be silent and let them finish whatever reason they believe they have to justify detaining you. Do not do anything to allow them to justify detention to become a

situation where it develops into probable cause for them to search or arrest.

- You have the right to an attorney once you are legally under arrest. Once you are made aware that you are under arrest, request immediately for your right to counsel.
- Regardless of your immigration status (if you have a green card, a visa, or do not have any status at all), even if you are not a citizen of the United States with full citizenship status, you still have constitutional rights. Do not be led to believe that because you are not a citizen these same principles do not apply to you.

CHAPTER 9

FREQUENTLY ASKED QUESTIONS (FAQS)

1. **Why Can Talking To The Police Be A Huge Problem For Someone's Criminal Case?**

There is a YouTube series posted by a Harvard professor that addresses this in brilliant fashion. It is around two hours long, but well worth taking the time to listen to. It is incredibly informative and gives both an academic and practical approach to why it is never advantageous to give voluntary statements to the police. In my opinion, there are a few exceptions to this, most notably in federal cases where one can actually benefit from engaging in certain types of cooperation. Other than this - there are very few situations where it can be produced to give a statement to the police; however, there are a host of reasons why it can be severely detrimental to an individual and their case.

2. Should You Talk When Confronted By Police?

You should never make any statements or interviews, or answer any questions (regardless of how formal or informal they may tell you they will be) without first getting advice from your attorney, nor should you do anything other than invoke your right to remain silent. Simply put, never speak to the police, a district attorney, an investigator, or any other individual who represents a law enforcement entity without the advice, counsel, and presence of your attorney. If the police convey to you directly how they are investigating a crime, and they express their desire to speak to you to ask questions related to the matter, you should respond very politely and with respect but also make very clear and without any equivocation how you have no intention of ever speaking about this matter without your criminal defense lawyer.

Remember: What You Say Can AND WILL Be Used Against You

Over and over again, you can hear cops on TV telling people that anything they say can and will be used against them in a court of law. This is absolutely accurate. Take heed of this advice and keep quiet. Keep in mind, this simple advice may seem easy in theory, but it may not prove so easy in practice. Police are schooled in interrogation techniques. Some cops are artists at figuring out ways to get suspects to make statements that they consider to be confessions.

A common scenario for why it is good practice to say as little as possible during police encounters would be during routine DWI investigations. In each criminal case, the state has to prove every element of the criminal charge beyond a reasonable doubt. Often, they may fail to be able to do so even with what seem to be very common or routine elements.

For example, charges of Driving While Intoxicated in Texas require the state to prove that an individual was actually "operating" a motor vehicle in a public place while intoxicated. Many times, they can't prove that the person was operating the motor vehicle without their own admission. Fortunately for prosecutors, admissions often come after people are asked what seem to be very benign questions by the police officer investigating the incident. Often, a police officer who is dispatched to investigate a possible individual for a charge of DWI will arrive after the fact, perhaps when the person is not even driving. In most scenarios where this occurs, almost all people usually just admit to the element of the operation. The officer asks what seem to be routine questions such as, "Where were you going? Or, "Where were you coming from?" Usually, people respond to this question, but by doing so they are implicitly admitting to the "operation" of the vehicle. If they instead do not answer ANY questions posed to them, it is possible the state might not be able to prove an element of the offense in order to gain a conviction.

Another situation exists when an individual may receive a call from a police officer claiming they are investigating a crime and want them to come down to the station and answer just a few "routine questions." Even if you're not guilty of whatever they are investigating a person for, usually they already have made the determination of if they will be arrested, so complying with their request is absolutely futile. All one would be doing, in essence, is providing the police with further ammunition to possibly use as evidence later in court.

When a person does comply with the request, it is usually because they want the opportunity to try and explain to the police officer what the factual scenario was, perhaps in the hope they can talk their way out of it, or make them understand it from their own point of view. Regardless, if this situation presents itself - one will only be making it worse for them, as the investigating police officer usually is only seeking to just verify whatever information he already suspects and to hopefully gain more.

Even very benign and simple statements that do not seem important may lead to an admission of some element of whatever crime they are investigating, such as admitting you were in the place where the crime occurred. It is possible that this is something they may not have been able to prove otherwise but for you admitting to being at or near the scene of the alleged incident or crime.

Police officers do not write the details of the facts in a manner that is in the person's favor giving the statement – or even in the way you may actually be telling them when explaining whatever may have occurred. Instead, they will undoubtedly write it in a narrative fashion in a manner and form of how best to prove whatever the charges may be alleged against the person. A statement such as "I went to his house to pick her up, and we went to go see a movie." The police report will instead write something to the effect of "the suspect admitted to being on the premises." Simply put, there is no winning, and one should avoid giving any statements to the police. Often people do so and are urged to explain their side of the events, but almost without fail, this will not yield the desired results and, in all likelihood, will somehow hurt their case and chance of obtaining a favorable result later in court.

Remember: Police Will Try to Trick You Into Talking

For years now, I have watched interrogation videos in awe. Even extremely intelligent people make the mistake of talking with the police. Believe it or not, even some of the best criminal defense attorneys have made the mistake of talking to the police, figuring that if they could just explain their side of things, the officer would let them go.

No matter how nice a police officer may seem, you must assume that they are trying to get information with which they can convict you. Do not fall for the nice guy routine. Remember, the courts have repeatedly held that the police have the right to lie. The only thing you need to say is that you want your lawyer.

Remember: Police May Try to Bully You Into Talking

Not all police interrogations are friendly question-and-answer sessions. Some can be downright hostile. But one thing remains the same. There is not one single thing that you need to discuss your case with the police or anyone else, for that matter, with the exception of your lawyer. Even if you find yourself in a raw interrogation that feels like you have no choice but to answer the officer's questions, you should still politely decline and say in no equivocal terms, "I want my lawyer."

3. Do Police Officers Have To Show ID?

It depends. Police officers who are undercover and working in plain clothes must identify themselves when exercising their police powers. However, a police officer in plain clothes is not ever required to identify themselves on demand and may even lie about them even being a police officer in some situations. If a police officer working in plain clothes wants to utilize their authority as a peace officer in certain situations such as when they are attempting to make an arrest, initiate a search, or demand that a citizen move on, they would have to provide their identity and that they are a police officer.

A police officer – like any member of society – can knock on your front door without announcing who they are. However, police officers seeking to search a residence with a search warrant are required to "knock and announce" meaning they must knock on the door or ring the doorbell and identify themselves as law enforcement with a search warrant. This rule was created by the courts to avoid the potential for violence that would be presented by officers simply forcing their way into a house without alerting the occupants to the lawful purpose being affected.

What's more, law enforcement officers are not always required to show identification upon request.

If you're pulled over in Texas, the only thing that you're required to do is give the officer either your name or your identifying information, which is usually your license. The officer, on the other hand, does not have to give you anything. If they are in uniform, they just have to tell you their name, rank, and station. If the officer does not tell you, ASK.

4. Will My Case Be Dropped Or Dismissed If The Police Do Not Read Me My Miranda Rights?

I get asked this question about Miranda rights very often. Unfortunately, the answer is usually no on almost every count. You will not be released from jail based on the fact that you were not read your rights. At the most, failure to have your Miranda rights read may result in a particular statement becoming inadmissible in court. In no way does it result in a case being dismissed or a suspect being released. There is a law, however, stating that you should be arraigned by a magistrate judge within 48 hours of arrest, which would apprise you of those rights.

5. Can The Police Lie To Me?

Yes. Police can, will, and often do lie -- especially if it helps them make arrests. One obvious example of this is when undercover officers claim not to be police. The rules regarding entrapment usually tip in favor of law enforcement, so the police won't hesitate to trick you into incriminating yourself or others. This is particularly common during interrogations in which officers might tell you that "your friend already gave you up, so you might as well come clean."

Supreme Court decisions have firmly established the right of law enforcement officials to lie to suspects, even about whether or not they are police officers. Entrapment is against the law, but lying about being a police officer does not constitute entrapment. The best defense against these manipulative tactics is to simply avoid saying anything to the police without first speaking with an attorney.

6. Should I Come To The Police Station Regarding An Incident?

If you're called to come down to give a statement about anything, you should hire an attorney immediately. Many people wait weeks before they finally hire an attorney and then respond to the police. If the case goes to trial with the detective testifying, he will reveal that it took several weeks to get the defendant to answer their questions. You should hire an attorney, and under no circumstance should you give a statement by yourself.

In most scenarios, it is even a bad idea to go give a statement with your attorney present. Some very good attorneys will refuse to take a case if a client insists on going down and giving a statement. They don't want to be the attorney who is sitting there while their clients are giving a confession. It's almost never advisable to go give a statement. Most people do because they think they can talk their way out of it. They can't.

7. **Why Should I Not Answer Questions If I Have Nothing To Hide? Isn't Refusing To Let The Police Question Or Search Me An Admission Of Guilt?**

No. If a police officer asks your permission to search, you are under no obligation to consent. The main reason why officers ask is that they don't have enough evidence to search without your consent. If you consent to a search request you give up one of the most important constitutional rights you have -- your Fourth Amendment protection against unreasonable searches and seizures.

A majority of avoidable police searches occur because citizens naively waive their Fourth Amendment rights by consenting to warrantless searches. As a general rule, if a person consents to a warrantless search, the search automatically becomes legal. Consequently, whatever an officer finds during such a search can be used to convict the person.

Don't expect a police officer to tell you about your right not to consent. Police officers are not required by law to inform you of your rights before asking you to consent to a search. In addition, police are prepared to use their authority to get people to consent to searches, and most people are predisposed to comply with any request an officer makes. For example, the average motorist stopped by an officer who asks them, "Would you mind if I search your vehicle, please?" will probably consent to the officer's search without realizing that they have every right to deny the request.

If you don't want the officer digging through your belongings, you should refuse to consent by saying something like, "Yes, I do mind. I have private, personal items in my [car, backpack, etc.] and do not want you looking through them." If the officer still proceeds to search you and finds illegal contraband, your attorney can argue that the contraband was discovered through an illegal search and should be thrown out of court.

You should never hesitate to assert your constitutional rights. Just say, "NO!

8. **If I'm Not Doing Anything Illegal, Why Shouldn't I Let The Police Search Me?**

The sad fact is that most people believe that they are under some kind of obligation to acquiesce when an officer contacts them and asks permission to search them or their belongings.

The truth is the exact opposite: You have a right to associate with and speak to whomever you please. In this respect, there is nothing special about a police officer. Assuming you would not let a complete stranger look through your purse or search your pockets, why would you allow a police officer to do so? Especially if you're not doing anything illegal! Just say, "NO!" to unwarranted searches.

9. **When Can the Police Legally Order Me To Exit My Vehicle?**

A police officer can order you to exit your vehicle at any time. If you're pulled over, the officer's first question will usually be whether you know why you were pulled over. You should not respond with an admission of any kind. Sometimes, they pull people over for no real reason. If you give them an answer, you've just given them the reasonable suspicion they need for an encounter to take place. If they have reasonable suspicion to detain you, they can ask you to get out of the vehicle for literally any reason.

10. What Are An Individual's Rights During A Traffic Stop?

In any police encounter, the number one rule is not to give statements. The more you talk, the worse it's going to be for you. I can't tell you how many cases I've handled where people have talked their way into a conviction, especially in a DWI case.

If an officer asks if you know why he pulled you over, you shouldn't guess. You should say no and let them articulate what the reason was for pulling you over. If they get you out of the vehicle, which they're legally entitled to do, and you feel like they are about to conduct an investigation for DWI by doing the sobriety tests, you should refuse. It's not a bad idea to ask the officer to clarify what the reason was for pulling you over. He doesn't have to answer you, but if he does and answers inconsistently, it could help your case.

11. Don't They Have To Read Me My Rights?

Many people believe that an officer must automatically read a person his or her Miranda rights as part of performing an arrest, either immediately before or immediately after an arrest is made. Consequently, many people believe that they can "beat the case" if the officer doesn't read them their Miranda rights during an arrest. This is a myth.

The only time an officer must read a person his or her Miranda rights is when: (1) the person has been placed under arrest AND (2) the officer is about to question the person about a crime. For example, if you're placed under arrest after consenting to a search request and confessing to ownership of found contraband, police do not need to read you your rights unless they want to question you about an unrelated crime.

If you're arrested, don't rely on the police to inform you of your right to remain silent and see a lawyer. It's up to you to assert those rights. Tell them, "I'm exercising my right to remain silent, and I would like to see a lawyer." If police persist in questioning you, repeat those magic words. The courts have made it clear that police officers do not have to tell people that they can refuse to consent to a warrantless search. In other words, a police officer does not need to read your rights before asking you to consent to a search.

Police officers are often pretty tricky about trying to get someone's consent to a search. They know that most people feel intimidated by police officers and are predisposed to comply with any request the police officer may make. For example, the average motorist stopped by a police officer who asks, "Would you mind opening the trunk, please?" will probably consent to the officer's search without realizing that they have every right to deny the officer's request. The courts have made clear that police do not have to tell you about your right to refuse searches. Also, despite the myth to the contrary, an officer does not need to get your consent in writing; oral consent is completely valid.

Remember that anything you say can and will be used against you in court. So don't try to talk yourself out of the situation, and don't make small talk with the police either.

12. When Will I See A Judge?

Article 15.17 of the Texas Code of Criminal Procedure states how a police officer who makes an arrest or who has custody of an arrested person shall "unnecessary delay, but no later than 48 hours after the person is arrested, take the person arrested or have him taken before some magistrate of the county where the accused was arrested or if it is more expeditious, to a magistrate in any other county of this state. In effect, then, even if you are not allowed to speak to an attorney after invoking the request to have one present, you should see a magistrate within 48 hours of the arrest. Generally speaking, the magistrate will then inform the individual of many of the rights that are enervated in the common Miranda warnings seen on TV, such as the right to counsel, how a lawyer will be appointed if the person is deemed to be indigent, they will inform them of the nature of the charge and accusation against them, etc.

13. What If A Police Officer Says He Will Go Easy On Me?

Unfortunately, many people get fooled by some version of this commonly used police officer's line: "Everything will be easier if you just cooperate." That's true to some extent -- it will make things much easier for the police officer who's trying to arrest you! But when it comes to you consenting to searches and answering incriminating questions, it couldn't be further from the truth.

Remember, the police will lie to you in order to get their way. Police are under no obligation to follow through on their promises, even if you hold up your end of the bargain by cooperating. Cooperating only increases the chances that you will incriminate yourself while having no effect on criminal sanctions. One thing is certain: Cooperating with someone who is trying to arrest you... just might get you arrested!

14. Can I Record The Police Encounter?

You are within your rights to record an encounter with the police, and in my opinion, you should. You can't obstruct their investigation, but recording them can make them go through the right protocol because it's no longer your word against theirs. In all police encounters, be polite, even when you're invoking your rights. It may mean the difference between a mere traffic ticket and a misdemeanor charge. When in outdoor public spaces where you are legally present, you have the right to capture any image that is in plain view. That includes pictures and videos of federal buildings, transportation facilities (including airports), and police officers.

- When you are on private property, the property owner sets the rules about the taking of photographs or videos. If you disobey property owners' rules, they can order you off their property (and have you arrested for trespassing if you do not comply).
- Police should not order you to stop taking pictures or video. Under no circumstances should they demand that you delete your photographs or video.

- Police officers may order citizens to cease activities that are truly interfering with legitimate law enforcement operations. In general, a court will trust an officer's judgment about what is "interfering" more than yours. So if an officer orders you to stand back, do so.
- If the officer says he or she will arrest you if you continue to use your camera, in most circumstances, it is better to put the camera away and call an attorney for help rather than risk being placed under arrest.
- Police officers may not generally confiscate or demand to view your photographs or video without a warrant. If you are arrested, the contents of your phone may be scrutinized by the police, although their constitutional power to do so remains unsettled. In addition, it is possible that courts may approve the seizure of a camera in some circumstances if police have a reasonable, good-faith belief that it contains evidence of a crime by someone other than the police themselves.

Using A Video Recorder (Including Cell Phones) With Audio Capacity

- You have a right to capture images in public places, but you don't always have a right to record what people say.
- You have the right to videotape and audiotape police officers performing official duties in public. That means you can record an officer during a traffic stop, during an interrogation, or while he or she is making an arrest.
- You can record people protesting or giving speeches in public.

If You Are Stopped Or Detained For Taking Photographs Or Videos

- Always remain polite and never physically resist a police officer.
- If stopped or you feel threatened by a police officer for taking photographs or videos, ask if you are free to go. If the officer says no, then you are being detained, something an officer cannot do without reasonable suspicion that

you have or are about to commit a crime or are in the process of doing so. Until you ask to leave, you are being stopped is considered voluntary under the law and is legal.

- If you are detained, politely state that you believe you have the right to take pictures or video and that you do not consent to the officer looking through or deleting anything on your camera. But if the officer reaches for your camera or phone, do not resist. Simply repeat that you do not consent to any search or seizure. You don't want to invite a charge for "resisting arrest."

15. Do I Have To Answer Questions If I Have Been Arrested?

If you are arrested, you do not have to answer any questions or volunteer any information. Ask for a lawyer right away. Repeat this request to every officer who tries to talk to or question you. You should always talk to a lawyer before you decide to answer any questions.

According to the Justice Robert Jackson, Nuremberg Prosecutor, Supreme Court Justice:

"*Any lawyer worth his salt will tell the suspect in no uncertain terms to make no statement to the police under any circumstances.*" ***Watts v. Indiana, 338 U.S. 49***

Types Of Things The Police Might Tell You To Get You To Talk To Them:

- "If you don't answer my questions, I'll have no choice but to arrest you. Do you want to go to jail?" (They will arrest you either way.)
- "You're not a suspect - just help us understand what happened here, and then you can go." (They will arrest you after you talk.)
- "If you don't answer my questions, I'm going to charge you with resisting arrest." (They will arrest you either way)
- "All of your friends have cooperated, and we let them go home. You're the only one left." (They will arrest you either way.)
- "You are just here voluntarily, and we appreciate you helping us with this. You are

free to leave at any time." (If you try to leave, they arrest you.)

I recently heard Professor James J. Duane talk about the perils of talking to the police. He was accompanied by a former police officer. This is some of what he had to say in my continuing education program…

Cops are sneaky, and there are lots of ways they can trick you into talking. They are allowed, even trained, to lie to you. Here are some cons they sometimes try to pull:

- Good Cop/Bad Cop: Bad cop is aggressive and menacing, while a good cop is nice, friendly, and familiar (usually a good cop is the same race and gender as you). The idea is that a bad cop scares you so bad you are desperately looking for a friend. A good cop is that friend until you are done talking.
- The cops will tell you that your friends ratted on you so that you will snitch on them. Meanwhile,

they tell your friends the same thing. If anyone breaks and talks, you all go down.

- The cops will tell you that they have all the evidence they need to convict you and that if you "take responsibility" and confess the judge will be impressed by your honesty and go easy on you. What they really mean is: "We don't have enough evidence yet, please confess."
- The cops may show you something and claim it is your fingerprints or tell you they have your fingerprints.
- The cops may tell you that they have you on video committing a crime. There may or may not be a video. It may or may not be someone who looks like you.
- Even if the cop questioning you is completely honest, that person is human and hears what he or she expects to hear. Jail is a very isolating and intimidating place. It is really easy to believe what the cops tell you. Insist upon speaking with a lawyer before you answer any questions or sign anything.

16. Do I Have To Go With A Police Officer?

You do not have to go with a police officer unless you are arrested, but there is a law that states you must go with them if you have witnessed a breach of the peace.

The police can arrest you solely to question you if they believe that you have broken or are breaking the law. If you are arrested for questioning, you still do not have to answer any questions except to give your correct name, address, and age.

CHAPTER 10

COMMON MYTHS

- **Myth #1: Police Cannot Lie During Questioning**

People often wonder and ask me if police are allowed to lie to a person during questioning. The answer is the police are absolutely allowed to lie to a person and routinely do so. The Reid Technique is the common interrogation technique detectives are taught to utilize when conducting an interrogation on a suspect. This technique was initially developed by John E. Reid in the mid-1900s and was revised by

Reid and Northwestern Law professor Fred Inbau in the 1962 book *Criminal Interrogations and Confessions,* which has been republished several times over the years. The "Reid Technique" is widely known as the bible of modern interrogations.

The Reid Technique has a basic premise of hurling intimidating threats and promises that are not legal or binding, and which the interrogator has no intention of honoring. The Reid Technique utilizes a method that involves three stages meant to break down a suspect's defenses and rebuild him back as a confessor.

First, the suspect is brought into custody and isolated from his familiar surroundings. This was the birth of the modern interrogation room, and how it is usually very small, not lit very well, and with no windows and little to no furniture or other items in the rooms, such as pictures on the wall, etc. A prime example of when the Reid technique was utilized was presented in the famous documentary on Netflix, *Making a Murderer*. The case included Brendan Dassey, a minor who confessed to a murder that he and his uncle may or may not have committed.

The detectives obtained the confession from the minor Brendan Dassey, which was the main piece of evidence used at trial through the implementation of the Reid technique. In the documentary, the youth gave a confession that was contradictory in nature, with certain facts stated that could not have been the actual case. After the interrogation is conducted, the young Dassey asks if he can have soda water to drink and when he will be allowed to go back to his gym class. Little did he know that what he just did was confess to a crime that would lead to his incarceration for the better part of his life.

At the very least, it's a very unreliable way to get information from someone because you are outright telling lies to a person about any number of things. I once heard Dean Strang, the main attorney involved in the case documented in *Making a Murderer*, speak at a forum in Dallas, Texas. There, he outlined the reasons for why he very much disagrees with the Reid technique, if for no other reason than because it commonly produces a confession that is inconsistent, unreliable, and not able to be fully trusted as the truth. When commenting on the Reid Technique, after remarking and detailing all of the details that were fraught with inconsistencies with the statement Brendan Dassey made with his statement, I remember he said it was first used in the early 1900s, and back then, there were United States Supreme Court opinions where way back then it noted how the Reid Technique was a preferable method to the alternative technique of simply and quite literally physically beating a confession from suspects.

At one point in time, I presume after hearing Mr. Strang speak, around a century ago, it was common for police officers to use physical force to beat someone until they gave the right confession sought. Confessions given under those circumstances were, of course, and obviously, very unreliable. The risk of a false confession with the Reid technique, however, is extremely high, even without the use of physical force. In this modern-day time, certainly, an alternate method could be employed or explored as an alternative to literally lying and playing mind games with people solely to get whatever admission they are trying to obtain.

- **Myth #2: They Have To Tell Me They Are The Police**

This is not true in the least. In fact, it is perfectly legal in most jurisdictions. It is a common myth, and misconception people believe that if an undercover officer is asked if they are a police officer, they must respond with the truth. This is a common and very prevalent myth. Police officers do NOT have to reveal their identity as cops, even if you ask them directly. Law enforcement officers are allowed to lie in order to make an arrest. They are taught how to lie. The courts have sanctioned police lying to suspects. That's what undercover operations are all about. Undercover means acting in an unofficial capacity or on assignment in a non-police capacity to most officers. For many of my clients, undercover means an officer is not wearing an official police uniform or without any identifiable police markings openly visible.

One exception, in theory, would be entrapment. In essence, entrapment is a situation where the police apply some form of persuasion to induce a person to commit a crime, where the individual likely had no predisposition to commit the offense otherwise. However, police officers can and do often pose undercover, and when doing this, they often provide a person with the "opportunity" to buy drugs but do not utilize or apply force or intimidation to convince one to do so. If the situation happens to be one where an individual is approached by an undercover police officer (or another agent for law enforcement), and they offer to sell an individual illegal narcotics, but the offer is refused, they still repeatedly come back and urge one to make the purchase. Usually, it would involve some form of pressure or threats, and in this event, it might be construed as entrapment which would invalidate the arrest and result in possibly the charges being dismissed. However, regardless - the common myth that if an undercover police officer is asked if he works for law enforcement he must be truthful is absolutely FALSE.

- **Myth #3: My Case Will Be Dismissed Or Thrown Out Because They Did Not Read Me My Miranda Rights.**

While the media on TV usually depicts police officers reading a suspect their Miranda rights right after an arrest, this is not necessarily always the case, and there is no requirement when it should be read. Regardless, even if it is not read, it will not lead to a dismissal. If you are ever placed under arrest for any criminal charge, the officer should read you your Miranda rights at some point. However, it is a common misconception that they are required to read a person their Miranda rights, which is not true. Usually, they do; in most cases, before a person is booked into jail, read them the basic Miranda rights, but there is no set time period or a specific juncture for when they are supposed to do so.

It's a mistaken belief that right after arrest, an officer must immediately read a person their Miranda rights, and in the event they do not - many people erroneously believe this somehow could lead to a positive result, like a dismissal or the charges being dropped. Miranda, in effect, really only comes into play as a relevant portion of a criminal charge if a suspect is NOT informed of these rights before law enforcement officials intend to interrogate and question them. If a person is under lawful arrest but Miranda rights are not read, any statement made would not be able to be used later in a proceeding in court. In fact, if no interrogation is conducted, then criminal prosecution can proceed even if a suspect has not ever been read their Miranda rights.

In order for Miranda to apply, you must be found to be in custody, meaning that the evidence was gathered at a time when you were either under arrest or your freedom of movement was restrained such that a reasonable person would not have felt free to leave. In addition, the evidence must either have been a product of interrogation or conduct that was similar in quality to interrogation, and it must have been conducted by a law enforcement official. If you are formally arrested, you are in custody. If you are not formally arrested, the custody answer is not so clear. If your freedom of movement is restricted by law enforcement, the question is whether a "reasonable person" would believe they are under arrest. If an officer stops you momentarily while you are driving or walking, you are likely not in custody for the purposes of Miranda.

Similarly, you are not considered to be in custody if you voluntarily agree to engage, talk, and/or interact with police officers by going to a police station and answering questions if at that time you were aware that you were free to leave if you so choose to just get up, leave, and walk away. If you are in custody and police officers interrogate you without reading you your Miranda rights, and if you answer their questions and your attorney can prove this assertion to be true, then any incriminating statements made would likely be ruled inadmissible for use in any hearings or at a trial. Simply put, the myth that because you believe after an arrest, it is an automatic "get out of jail free" card" is an erroneous belief.

- **Myth #4: There Is No Forensic DNA Or Fingerprint Evidence, So I Cannot Be Convicted Of A Crime.**

While forensic evidence such as DNA or fingerprint evidence can significantly be an advantage for the prosecution in any criminal case, it is by no means exclusively necessary in order to obtain a conviction. In fact, the majority of criminal convictions are typically based on circumstantial evidence and witness testimony at trial, often either through the testimony of a police officer or an eyewitness to the incident.

People love to watch CSI and sometimes believe everything on the show regarding forensic evidence and how strong the merits of it are in relation to a criminal case does not necessarily apply in reality in actual criminal cases and trials. The assumption that police officers, investigators, and prosecutors only solve crimes by using some type of forensic evidence is a myth many people believe. While forensic evidence such as fingerprint analysis, voice recognition, or DNA specimens can help increase the odds of a conviction, it is not something that is absolutely required in order for someone to be convicted of a crime.

Many people do believe the myth that without such forensic evidence being present, a defendant cannot be convicted. However, this belief is entirely wrong and far from true. A great majority of criminal cases do not involve any forensic or scientific evidence of any kind and rely solely on the testimony of witnesses, police officers, experts, and criminal investigators. In fact, the testimony of just a single witness (sometimes referred to as the one witness rule) of someone such as a single police officer who investigated the case or an alleged victim or complaining witness to the crime, can be enough is usually enough for the prosecution to seek to obtain a conviction (assuming the trier of fact believes their testimony as proof beyond a reasonable doubt).

The popular depiction of scientific experts giving very intricate and complex testimony regarding the validity of certain pieces of evidence or the notion that technicians will testify who performed a very complicated analysis of a crime scene is indeed portions introduced as evidence at criminal trials. However, in many instances, this type of testimony and the complexity associated with it is usually the exception and not the norm.

- **Myth #5: I Was Not In The Car, Or I Left The Scene So I Cannot Be Charged With Possession.**

People often believe that if certain illegal items, such as illicit narcotics, are not directly found on a person, they cannot be charged with the criminal offense of possession of a controlled substance nor convicted of the crime at trial. Very often, I hear people say how they should get an instant dismissal and fervently point out how because they did not find any of the drugs in question on them, the charges are bogus, and the police officer made a huge mistake.

This is not true, and the proposition of the legal nature of what it proposes is far from what is true in reality. Possession involves the exercise of control, management, care, custody, or control over a substance or contraband. Possession of illegal substances can be classified as either "active" or "constructive."

Possession of the illegal substance would be categorized as "active" when it is clearly found on or near a person or when it is clear they were aware of its presence and, either individually or in conjunction with other parties, had the ability to exercise power and intent to control its disposition or use. Active possession would be a scenario where you physically have something illegal on your person, such as in your pocket, in your jacket, in your car, or purse. Constructive possession, on the other hand, exists when you do not have actual possession, but still, have the intent and capability to maintain control and dominion over the contraband. Possession can be constructive when an individual has the ability to exercise some form of control over (such as in a passenger seat while someone else is driving the car).

There is a very distinct difference between “actual possession” and “constructive possession.”

Constructive possession refers to a scenario where you may not be in actual physical contact with something contraband, but you may know where they are and have the ability to control and move them. Constructive possession identifies a situation in which you don't have bodily contact with the container or drug that the drug is in; however, you still understand where they are, and you are in charge of those. This includes knowingly concealing them in your residence or automobile. Possession can also be constructive when an individual has the ability to control the object (e.g., in the passenger seat while the individual is operating the motor vehicle).

Presence, accessibility, and proximity are among several issues that may be sufficient to establish possession. Constructive possession can only exist if there is some knowledge the contraband was found in a place on or around your property and one had the capability to maintain dominion and control over it. Constructive possession can be sole or joint, meaning either an individual or a group of a few individuals can be charged using constructively possessing the exact same controlled substance. For instance, two people residing in the same home where just one bag of marijuana is found can both be held accountable for constructively owning the single bag.

Circumstances that can lead to a finding of constructive possession include:

1. When a police officer watches a person drop what they later found to be illegal contraband.
2. Your mere location and proximity to the illegal contraband.
3. Whether one owned or occupied the location where drugs were found.
4. Where one clearly had control of the item in which the illegal contraband was located.
5. Where one had the opportunity, or lack thereof, to move or dispose of the drugs where they were found.
6. Where one had any personal belongings at the location where the illegal contraband was found.
7. Where one either fled or engaged in other suspicious behavior.

8. Where one was engaged in drug activity or was otherwise impaired.

The overall rationale, in totality, is if the state can prove an individual had a nexus or a close tie to the illegal contraband when it was found by law enforcement, one could be charged and possibly convicted of a "possession" charge.

- **Myth #6: The Victim Does Not Want To Press Charges Against Me.**

The idea of any individual "pressing charges," regardless of whether or not they wanton individual is prosecuted or not, is indeed perhaps one of the single most misconstrued notions when it comes to criminal law cases, especially in assault charges. The general concept is very simplistic in nature: Any individual or person can choose to, or refuse, to have someone charged and prosecuted for a criminal offense, and if they are the alleged victim in the case, they have the ultimate power and authority to ensure all charges are dropped.

While it is true that DAs may be less likely to aggressively pursue charges in this context, it is usually because they are weighing the strength and merits of the case and determining the worth of the case and evidence considering how a material witness seems unwilling to cooperate with an investigation and has expressed the desire for the charge to be dropped. However, it should be perfectly clear that any individual, even if they are the complaining witness or a victim in a case, simply does not have the power or authority on their own to make sure certain charges do not get filed or are dropped. This is actually far from true, and actually, the contrary proposition in many situations seems to exist.

Ultimately, the overall determination of whether an individual is charged and prosecuted for any given crime is always and ONLY up to the prosecutor assigned to the case. Prosecutors have a very wide amount of leeway and discretion in the specific types of charges they intend to pursue, file, and prosecute, and the ultimate decision is only up to them and THEM ALONE. An individual, even if they are a complaining witness or a victim in a case, has literally almost no control over the decision that will be made by the assigned prosecutor of the case. Furthermore, citizens typically cannot file criminal charges on their own, nor can they stop prosecutors from filing criminal charges. After an arrest has been made, it is entirely out of the victim's hands as to what will happen in court. This can be a frustrating proposition - after all, they are the ones who made the initial call for the arrest, right? They should have the authority, then, to dictate what happens to the person for whom they made the original complaint. Right? Wrong.

Actually, when victims constantly contact authorities to get charges dropped, it can actually lead to a worse result. Why? Often, if a victim persists in trying to get charges dropped against their loved one, prosecutors may go into a "reactive" or “protective" mode because they believe the person is being pressured into doing this for some reason. The reasons could vary; maybe they don't want to see their spouse go to jail, maybe the spouse is pressuring them to make the call to the DA's office in hopes the charges will be dropped, and they won't have to go to court, go to trial, be placed on probation, or in some cases go to jail or prison.

The logic is it could be the case where a battered spouse testifies to help get their loved one out of trouble, only to be harmed perhaps worse in the future. In essence, they are attempting to protect the battered spouse against themselves. Especially in a family violence case, the state can prosecute a defendant, and possibly obtain a conviction, with or without the assistance or wishes of the alleged complaining witness. Either way, often the DAs go into a reactive, or a protective mode, to protect the battered spouse, and not only will the charges NOT be dropped, but the case may also be prosecuted more vigorously against the individual than if the victim had not tried to drop the charges in the first place.

Simply put, regardless of the type of case, the victim DOES NOT have the power, or the authority, to make the decision to drop or to dismiss any pending charges. It is out of their hands, and usually within the sole discretion of whatever DA office is handling the matter.

- **Myth #7: "I Can Talk My Way Out Of This Situation."**

This is a common myth and misconception, and one that very often leads to individuals suspected of a crime who believe this notion of being true, making the overall evidence for their case much worse for themselves later when it proceeds to court. Police officers, detectives, investigators, etc., are all trained and very skilled in eliciting incriminating information from suspects. You will never talk yourself out of trouble; however, very often, you may put yourself in the position of talking your way into more trouble and, possibly, ultimately a conviction for the charge.

One of the basic tenets of Miranda rights, as everyone has heard on TV, is how one of the warnings given is when the arresting police officer states how "anything they say can and will be used against them later in court." They do not have this in the Miranda warnings to pay mere lip service, it is, in fact, one of the warnings enumerated in Miranda for a very good reason because they absolutely mean it when said.

The more you try and talk to a police officer about the alleged incident, what occurred, and what role you may have played in it, only will be used, granted often out of context and written in a different manner than intended when it was said, the more strength and leverage a prosecutor will have to be used as evidence against you later in court. Thus, it cannot be stated enough - ALWAYS, albeit politely, exercise your politely constitutional right to remain silent, and avoid making any possible incriminating statements. This is the only surefire method and the single best way to avoid making a situation altogether worse for you. I have seen it, from experience, time and time ago. YOU HAVE THE RIGHT TO REMAIN SILENT - SO USE IT!

- **Myth #8: A Person Will Be Better Off If They Cooperate.**

Many individuals mistakenly believe that they should fully cooperate with the police because they will be better or because they promised to go "easier on them" if they did. However, it is always important to remember that police are allowed to lie to a person to try and obtain what they want. Often, they will try to tell someone how if they just "cooperate, everything will go easier for you." And usually, will they make clear how if they do not and refuse to give their consent to search something (a vehicle), they may threaten the person.

The thing is, law enforcement officers have no obligation whatsoever to follow through with empty promises made; in fact, they rarely do. This is the case even where a person agrees and does what was asked on their end but soon will find out this will almost never be reciprocal, and they have agreed to do so by naively placing their trust in a police officer who will only make do this in order to freely obtain incriminating information. If a person doesn't immediately offer their consent, they may form a bit further try and put you at ease by saying if they agree to allow for the search or to answer questions, it will be much quicker and easier overall because he is only there to get them straightened out, and once this is ascertained will usually imply everyone can go on their way.

One should be almost more on guard whenever a police officer in a scenario such as this acts nicer than usual because they are doing so with the sole intent of making their job easier and to make yours worse. When a police officer is investigating a crime, they are not there to make friends or to just do a cursory search for what happened, or to play as if they are Columbo or Sherlock Holmes, and so on. Most people in this situation do not realize how this mind trick is done only to help make an arrest easier and with better evidence obtained as a result. It is a trick designed to take advantage of a trusting individual.

If you are being questioned about a crime and you believe you are likely one of the suspects, you must realize quickly how this ploy for information is done only because the police officer is seeking the easiest way to make an arrest, and unless one is steadfast and never provides the consent requested, it will not allow the officer for the quicker way in order to do his investigation, make his arrest, so he can be done with his work earlier and with doing much less work.

If one finds themselves in an encounter such as this, it is imperative to realize how the police officer is not your friend and has no care whatsoever about you, whether you get arrested, how this will affect your life, your family, or any possible ramification a person may face with employment and could care less if it will cause someone to lose their job and ability to provide income for a family. He is not your friend; he is not concerned for you, your family, nor where your next meal is coming from. One should immediately be concerned if this ultimately somehow is conveyed, and it is all the more important to remain steadfast in not giving any form of consent.

CHAPTER 11

WHY DO WE DO WHAT WE DO?

When someone learns of my profession, I am very often asked the question, "How do you defend those people?" It never ceases to amaze me how many people are disgusted that I would voluntarily choose to earn my living defending and representing a person accused of a crime by the police. Arrest increasingly means guilt, and there is a public perception of criminal defense attorneys as being somewhat unethical and disingenuous. Certainly, every criminal defense attorney has been asked many times at cocktail parties how they stomach representing criminals.

However, in my mind, the answer to this question is both complex and simplistic in nature. It involves having a passionate desire to protect the innocent from being unjustly accused of a crime, the amount of faulty and inaccurate evidence, wrongful convictions, overcharging by the prosecutor of a punishment more severe than meets the crime, protecting and safekeeping our fundamental constitutional rights, ensuring the fairness of proceedings at trial, and protection from unjust laws and overly harsh and possibly illegal punishment. My job is to keep the government honest, and without criminal defense attorneys to counterweight the balance, we would live in a virtual police state. A very good answer was stated once by the United States Supreme Court Justice Byron White in the case of United States vs. Wade, 388 U.S. 218 (1967):

"Law enforcement officers have the obligation to convict the guilty and to make sure they do not convict the innocent. They must be dedicated to making the criminal

trial a procedure for the ascertainment of the true facts surrounding the commission of the crime. To this extent, our so-called adversary system is not adversary at all; nor should it be. But defense counsel has no comparable obligation to ascertain or present the truth. Our system assigns him a different mission. He must be and is interested in preventing the conviction of the innocent, but, absent a voluntary plea of guilty, we also insist that he defend his client whether he is innocent or guilty. The State has the obligation to present the evidence. Defense counsel need present nothing, even if he knows what the truth is. He need not furnish any witnesses to the police, or reveal any confidences of his client, or furnish any other information to help the prosecution's case. If he can confuse a witness, even a truthful one, or make him appear at a disadvantage, unsure or indecisive, that will be his normal course. Our interest in not convicting the innocent permits counsel to put the State to its proof, to put the State's case in the worst possible light, regardless of what he thinks or knows to be the truth. Undoubtedly there are some limits that defense counsel must observe but more often than not, defense counsel will cross-examine a prosecution witness, and impeach him if he can, even if he thinks the witness is telling the truth, just as he will attempt to destroy a witness who he thinks is lying. In this respect, as part of our modified adversary system and as part of the duty imposed on the most honorable defense counsel, we countenance or require conduct which in many instances has little, if any, relation to the search for truth."

Possibly one day, you, or someone close to you, such as a friend or loved one, will be accused and arrested for a criminal offense. I can assure you that if that happens, regardless of guilt or innocence, you will want beyond all hope to find a competent attorney to represent them as a zealous advocate to defend them against the overwhelming force of the government.

AM I FREE TO LEAVE? (FLOW CHART I)

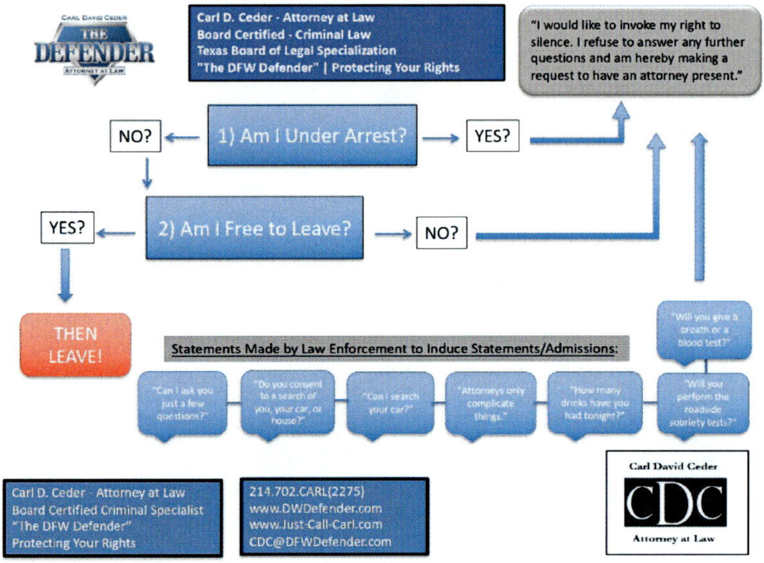

How To Deal With Police? (Flow Chart II)

HOW TO DEAL WITH POLICE

CHEAT SHEET

Stay Calm & Cool, be courteous | Film interactions, try to get names/badges if possible
NEVER CONSENT TO ANY SEARCHES | You are not required to talk to police or answer questions
Be polite, BUT FIRM | Ask "Are you detaining me?" and/or "Am I free to leave?"

QUESTION/COMMENT	WALKING	DRIVING	CHECK POINT
CAN I SEE YOUR ID?	Ask if you are being detained or if you are free to go and walk away. If you are detained, you are required to stay by law.	Carrying an ID is generally required if you are operating a motor vehicle.	Your constitutional rights still apply at checkpoints. Never roll down your window all the way down. Ask for supervisor if necessary.
CAN YOU FILM THE POLICE?	It is 100% legal to record the police.	Videotaping a police officer who pulled you over is legal.	Vide of TSA checkpoints is legal as long as you do not film the TSA's monitors, or interfere with or slow down the screening process.
MIND IF I TAKE A LOOK? (Consent)	DO NOT CONSENT TO A SEARCH.	DO NOT CONSENT TO A SEARCH.	DO NOT CONSENT TO A SEARCH.
WHERE ARE YOU GOING?	You have no legal duty to answer any questions, and you may refuse to answer and ignore.	You do not have to answer, but that can be met with suspicion and they might find a reason to give you a ticket. The main reason they ask this is to test you.	

INDEX

M

P

R

S

T

U

V

NOTES

Made in United States
North Haven, CT
05 November 2026

21763979R60106